STUDYING PSYCHOLO(

CW00507554

STUDYING PSYCHOLOGICAL SCIENCE

A guide to accompany
Bond and McConkey
Psychological science: An introduction

Darren Walton

The McGraw-Hill Companies, Inc.

Beijing Bogotà Boston Burr Ridge IL Caracas
Dubuque IA Lisbon London Madison WI
Madrid Mexico City Milan Montreal New Delhi
New York San Francisco Santiago Seoul
Singapore St Louis Sydney Taipei Toronto

Irwin/McGraw-Hill

A Division of The **McGraw·Hill** *Companies*

Copyright © 2001 McGraw-Hill Australia Pty Limited
Additional owners of copyright are named in on-page credits.

Apart from any fair dealing for the purposes of study, research, criticism or review, as permitted under the *Copyright Act*, no part may be reproduced by any process without written permission. Enquiries should be made to the publisher, marked for the attention of the Publishing Manager, at the address below.

Every effort has been made to trace and acknowledge copyright material. Should any infringement have occurred accidentally the authors and publishers tender their apologies.

Copying for educational purposes
Under the copying provisions of the *Copyright Act*, copies of parts of this book may be made by an educational institution. An agreement exists between the Copyright Agency Limited (CAL) and the relevant educational authority (Department of Education, University, VET, etc.) to pay a licence fee for such copying. It is not necessary to keep records of copying except where the relevant educational authority has undertaken to do so by agreement with the Copyright Agency Limited.

For further information on the CAL licence agreements with educational institutions, contact the Copyright Agency Limited, Level 19, 157 Liverpool Street, Sydney, NSW 2000. Where no such agreement exists, the copyright owner is entitled to claim payment in respect of any copies made.

National Library of Australia Cataloguing-in-Publication Data

Walton, Darren
Studying psychological science: a guide to accompany Bond and McConkey Psychological science: An introduction.

   Includes index
   ISBN 0 07 470825 2

   1. Psychology – Problems, exercises, etc. 2. Study skills.
   I. Title.

150

Published in Australia by
McGraw-Hill Australia Pty Limited
4 Barcoo Street, Roseville, NSW 2069, Australia
Acquisitions Editor: Jae Chung / Jennifer Speirs
Project Coordinator: Jo Munnelly / Jennifer Speirs
Editor: Carolyn Pike
Designer / typesetter: Jan Schmoeger, Designpoint
Printed by: Best Tri Colour Printing & Packaging Co. Ltd, Hong Kong

CONTENTS

About the author   ix

Preface   xi

Chapter 1 Aims of the Study Guide   1
Overview   1
1.1   The four requirements of Introductory Psychology   1
1.2   Structure of the Study Guide   2
1.3   This Guide and the World Wide Web   3
1.4   What's on the Bond and McConkey Web pages   3
1.5   Frequently asked questions and updates   4
1.6   This Guide and the APA Manual   4
1.7   Strategies for learning: *Psychological science:
       An introduction*   5

Chapter 2 Careers in Psychology   7
Overview   7
Introduction   7
2.1   Skills acquired in undergraduate Psychology   8
2.2   Clinical Psychology   10
2.3   Organisational Psychology   11
2.4   Academic Psychology   12
2.5   Counselling   13
2.6   Sports Psychology   14
2.7   Forensic Psychology   15
2.8   Educational and Developmental Psychology   15
2.9   Other uses for Psychology   16

Chapter 3   Essay writing in Psychology   **17**
    Overview   17
    3.1   An introduction to essay writing in Psychology   17
    3.2   The essay formula   20
    3.3   Refinements to the formula   24
    3.4   Essay style   36
    3.5   Things to avoid   37
    3.6   Referencing   43
    3.7   Essentials of the referencing formulae   45
    3.8   Frequently asked questions   46
    3.9   Eleven easy steps for researching and writing essays   50
    3.10   The essay checklist   53

Chapter 4   Research report writing   **57**
    Overview   57
    Introduction   57
    4.1   The research report formula   58
    4.2   Refinements to the formula for research report writing   60
    4.3   The introduction   61
    4.4   The hypothesis   62
    4.5   Methods: sample, materials and procedures   63
    4.6   Data presentation   65
    4.7   The discussion   70
    4.8   The abstract   72
    4.9   Things to avoid   73
    4.10   The research report checklist   76
    4.11   Frequently asked questions   77

Chapter 5   Appraising theory and arguments   **79**
    Overview   79
    5.1   How do theories function?   81
    5.2   The prime directive   81
    5.3   How to be critical effectively   82
    5.4   Developing your argument   84
    5.5   Avoiding fallacies   87
    5.6   How to avoid fallacies   95

Chapter 6   Finding and using resources   **97**
    Overview   97
    6.1   Terminology frustration   97
    6.2   Types of materials   98
    6.3   Lectures   107
    6.4   Frequently asked questions   108

Chapter 7   Dealing with statistics   **111**
Overview   111
Reducing fears about things statistical   111
7.1   Step 1 Starting out with statistics   113
7.2   Step 2 First statistics: mean, median, mode   116
7.3   Step 3 Analysing variability: z-scores   118
7.4   Step 4 Types of variables   122
7.5   Step 5 The Pearson product moment correlation
        coefficient   124
7.6   Step 6 The t-test   127
7.7   Approaching statistics examinations   132
7.8   Frequently asked questions   133
7.9   Answers to exercises   136

Chapter 8   Examinations   **143**
Overview   143
8.1   Four generalisations about Psychology examinations   144
8.2   Studying for examinations   146
8.3   Sitting examinations   146
8.4   Advice about examination anxiety   149
8.5   Frequently asked questions   151

Chapter 9   Epilogue   **153**
Overview   153
9.1   On becoming a psychologist   153
9.2   On making the decision to become a psychologist   154
9.3   A final note   155

References   157

Index   159

ABOUT THE AUTHOR

Darren Walton entered the University of Canterbury in 1988 and left in 1995 with a First Class BSc (Hons) and a PhD in Philosophical Psychology. For four years he taught Social Psychology and Physiological Psychology by distance at the Open Polytechnic of New Zealand. He has taught Psychology to managers, accountants, nurses, high school students and doctors—people of all ages and stages of life. He has tutored soldiers on exercise, navy personnel in the Mediterranean and those incarcerated in maximum security prisons. To cover the range of people and to consider the resources that different people bring to their study involves a special sort of experience. Previously he taught Developmental Psychology and first year laboratories at the University of Canterbury. Currently, Darren is employed by the Office of the Commissioner of the NZ Police in a human resources role.

PREFACE

My first year as a Psychology student was over 10 years ago at the University of Canterbury in Christchurch, New Zealand. Before writing this preface, I travelled to my old university to restore to mind all the memories of my first year of learning psychology. Remarkably enough the place had not changed in the four years I had been away. The laboratories where I learnt Psychology were the same and a new generation of students (like you) were studying the same things that I had learned years before. The library was the same, although the Psychology section had been moved. The student union had been re-renovated, amazingly, to operate almost the way it did when I was a first year. The lecture theatres were the same, although some new ones had been added. The professors looked almost the same. I knew the place well; it hadn't really changed at all. But despite the fact that nothing of substance had altered, I struggled to find anything in my old Psychology department to cue my memory of being a first year student.

On the last day of my visit it occurred to me that the university hadn't changed at all but that I had. In a 'eureka' kind of way, I realised exactly what it is to be a first year student, to do Psychology and to struggle to overcome the hurdles of university study.

This *Study Guide* is meant to help you overcome a whole range of hurdles—most importantly, what you should focus on when reading your text and how to use it for your writing, study and examinations. This Guide's philosophy is simple enough. The material here is designed to help you acquire the fundamentals of your study: how to write, what sort of things to read; hints on how to get through examinations; and what to ask and what not to be afraid of.

The *Study Guide* is pragmatic and its contents may not be entirely welcomed by lecturers who want you to extend yourself through your study. In offering shortcuts, you are not being offered a way to cheat through your introductory course but sometimes the advice will seem as if you are encouraged to just 'get it done the easy way' with the instruction that 'this is the way!'. This approach may seem to rob you of the opportunity to learn 'properly'. However, there are plenty of challenges at university and plenty of things in Psychology for you to be critical about that will absorb your intellectual potential. I hope you find those things and elect to develop a stance. The real task is to learn which things to challenge. The advice in this Guide is meant to make your studying the fundamentals easier. In this way, you can free up your opportunity to take on those things that you elect to pursue. That's your purpose, that's why you have started, and whether you know it instantly, or remember it in 10 years, that's what taking an introductory course in Psychology, or any other course, is all about.

The material in each of the chapters is reasonably condensed. This is a deliberate attempt to reach those fundamentals quickly. In the case of the guide to essay writing, in particular, a 100-page guide to essay writing confronts students like the complete guide to the rules of cricket confront those with a bat and a ball who just want to play the game. More poignant, perhaps, you can't become good at cricket by reading the rule book; it's all about practice. So, knowing something of tight deadlines and knowing that essay writing is an acquired skill, the guide to essay writing provides a lot of shortcuts in the hope that, by reading for an hour or so, you will grasp a lot of new things about the complexity of the writing in Psychology. It's worth the hour or so.

I hope the advice is helpful, although I cannot possibly predict all the problems you will encounter. Different lecturers and different departments will have different expectations. Each person who takes on Psychology will bring in their own experiences and seek out their own challenges to overcome, and gain their own rewards. Nonetheless, advice is offered on the most common sorts of problems people taking psychology need to overcome. By offering suggestions to cope with these problems, I have provided examples of good strategies that you can adopt for your own pursuits. Learning strategies to deal with your own hurdles is the aim of this Guide. I hope you find this Guide beneficial as you take on your challenges.

CHAPTER 1
AIMS OF THE *STUDY GUIDE*

OVERVIEW

1.1 The four requirements of Introductory Psychology
1.2 Structure of the *Study Guide*
1.3 This Guide and the World Wide Web
1.4 What's on the Bond and McConkey Web pages
1.5 Frequently asked questions and updates
1.6 This Guide and the APA Manual
1.7 A strategy for learning *Psychological science: An introduction*

1.1 The four requirements of Introductory Psychology

No matter where you study, any Introductory Psychology course will be designed for you to acquire four things:

1. the ability to write a formal essay in Psychology
2. the ability to carry out and present the results of a laboratory exercise
3. a basic understanding of statistics and the design of experimentation for psychological inquiry
4. a broad knowledge of the theories and research that define Psychology as a subject matter.

■

Commit yourself to quality from day one ... it's better to do nothing at all than to do something badly.
Mark H. McCormack

1

What resources do Psychology lecturers rely on to ensure you accomplish these tasks and how do they know whether you acquire a standard of proficiency? In the case of essay writing and laboratory reports, you will present your written material for inspection. The resources you will be given may include reading lists, lectures, tutorial support, the laboratories themselves, writing guides and a guide to referencing. In the case of statistics, you may get a resource book, a separate text, tutorials, and lectures—or perhaps you will be advised to take a course in statistics. You will probably sit an examination to test this sort of knowledge.

Acquiring a broad knowledge of the theories and research is achieved through two means–lectures and your textbook. The textbook covers more topics than your lectures will cover. Lectures are designed to extend components of your textbook and to develop a more detailed investigation of specific issues. In practice, it is your knowledge of the textbook that will feature prominently in your assessment. You will not learn all there is to know about Psychology by reading your textbook but it contains knowledge of the fundamentals of Psychology that will be built on if you progress through to higher levels of Psychology. Psychology lecturers usually rely on a textbook to carry you through to a level where your skills in researching, analysing and writing become more important than the knowledge you absorb by reading a textbook. But of prime importance to you, for now, is to know the textbook. It is a good idea to find out how well you know the textbook prior to an examination. It is also good to know how to use the textbook to assist you with essay writing, laboratory reports and the analysis of theory and evidence.

Knowing a textbook is not about just reading it, taking notes or even memorising it. You must be able to use the information in it, see the connections between subject materials and be able to respond to assessment on it without rigidly recalling only what the text states. It is the aim of this *Study Guide* to assist you in understanding the functions of the textbook, guide you through your assessments and offer you shortcuts for getting to those end goals of writing essays, writing reports, sitting examinations and understanding statistics. Thankfully, there are some shortcuts.

1.2 Structure of the *Study Guide*

Students prefer to be treated as capable learners who need a guide every now and then, not a set of rules. Students want to know what the rules are, but they don't want to find this out by being issued with a set of instructions. This Guide has been produced with this view in mind. For example, instead of providing lengthy accounts of the requirements for essay writing, material is provided to enable students to achieve the best grade possible.

This Guide is to be read and advantage taken of its advice. It is difficult to get students to read the traditional 50 000 word guide to writing essays when their aim is to write a 1000 word essay. Thus, Chapters 3 and 4 provide a scaffolding,

■

> Education is an admirable thing, but it is well to remember
> that nothing that is worth knowing can be taught.
>
> *Oscar Wilde*

a formula, which broadly outlines what is expected when writing essays and research reports. After each 'formula', there is advice on how to improve upon each component and the things to avoid, a checklist and a set of frequently asked questions with answers. Even the student who is pushed for time should benefit from the outlines and the checklists. However, students who take consideration of the suggested improvements to the formulae will accelerate their understanding of writing within Psychology and achieve better grades on their assignments.

1.3 This Guide and the World Wide Web

This Guide accompanies the textbook, *Psychological science: An introduction*, and a Web page accompanies this Guide. The purpose of the Web page is to provide practical examples, interactive exercises and links to material that may be helpful or informative. Multiple-choice examinations can be accessed to assess your knowledge of a chapter, the entire textbook or any combination of chapters. The Web page is interactive and thus is designed to accommodate those things that Web pages do very well, such as multiple-choice questions that are scored automatically, but print-based materials do poorly. In contrast, this Guide retains those things that would be difficult for you to manage on a computer screen, such as a guide to essay and laboratory report writing, advice on resources and so on.

The combination of the Web and the print material provides you with two valuable resources that are divided by their intended function. The print material provides the advice and guidance to your course of study; the Web material provides you with practice and extension. Thus, this *Study Guide* is designed to prepare you for tasks and help you carry them out. It offers the sort of guidance, shortcuts, hints and suggestions that you would get from having a tutor constantly available. You will not find the traditional self-assessments, test questions and numerous pages of multiple-choice questions. These questions are available on the Web pages. Because the Web page is interactive, you will get the benefit of scoring, feedback and hints on which areas you need to revise.

1.4 What's on the Bond and McConkey Web pages

On the Web page you'll find multiple-choice questions derived from each of the chapters. A special Internet interface, 'MaxMark', has been developed just for these multiple-choice questions. Each chapter has 30 or so multiple-choice questions for you to do, so that as you progress through with your study you can test your knowledge. You will get feedback on the answers in the form of reference back to the textbook, graphs or figures and sometimes an Internet link that will take you to a website that is useful for further developing your understanding. There are separate links to useful sites that contain information relevant to Psychology.

The link to the site is: www.mcgraw-hill.com.au/mhhe/psychology/bond/

■

> In theory, there is no difference between theory and practice. But, in practice, there is.
>
> *Jan L. A. van de Snepscheut*

1.5 Frequently asked questions and updates

Wherever possible, a list of frequently asked questions and some answers have been provided. As the Bond and McConkey Web page is capable of being updated, questions frequently asked by readers of this Guide will be answered there as well as a set of answers to assist with those questions not frequently encountered. If you have a general query you cannot find an answer for in this Guide, please contact the e-mail address on the Web page. If sufficient numbers of people ask the same questions, an answer will be provided and posted on the page under 'Updates'.

1.6 This Guide and the APA Manual

Lecturers and researchers also have a guide to help them write and present reports. The guide psychologists use is called the APA Manual, that is, the *Publication manual of the American Psychological Association* (APA, 1994). The APA Manual began in 1929 as seven pages outlining the formatting a psychologist should adopt when presenting journal articles. It has developed into a manual of more than 350 pages. The APA Manual is the definitive guide for referencing, formatting and structuring reports and essays for publication.

So, why don't lecturers direct you to the APA Manual to get you under way with your essays? Why bother with this Guide? Apart from the fact that this Guide offers much more than some guides to writing, there are two broad reasons why you are not directed to obtain a copy of the APA Manual at an introductory level. First, the Manual is meant for researchers writing for publication and much of what it contains will not apply to your immediate concerns. Writing for publication involves recognising a process of review and copy editing (the process of turning a manuscript into print). When you write your essays and reports you act as reviewer, proofreader, typesetter and publisher. You are engaged in a different sort of exercise. Second, the APA Manual is technical, lengthy and expensive. Absorbing the information in the APA Manual would be difficult without some basic experience in report writing. When you progress through Psychology you will become more and more familiar with it. Postgraduate students in Psychology are expected to follow the APA Manual.

This Guide offers the fundamentals of essay writing and is intended to accord with the prescriptions of the APA Manual. However, one particular piece of the APA Manual must be taken seriously for our purposes here. In the Foreword, the APA Manual makes two important statements. First, considering the style requirements, '... authors should balance the rules of the Publication Manual with good judgment' (APA, 1994, p. xxiii). Second, considering bias in language, the 'APA considers these specialised guidelines 'living documents ...'(APA, 1994, p. xxiii). These expressions indicate the spirit of the APA Manual and help resolve any difficulties you might encounter when lecturers and tutors provide an outline for an essay that does not quite accord with the APA Manual (or this Guide for that matter).

You can be a little flexible[1]: follow the instructions your lecturers provide and recognise the spirit of what the rules are intended to achieve. If you have a particular problem that does not have an answer in this Guide, you will probably find the answer in the APA Manual. If you still have difficulty, ask a tutor, or use your judgment, and if you want advice, post your concern on the Bond and McConkey Web page.

1.7 Strategies for learning: *Psychological science: An introduction*

The ability to write a formal essay

Read the sections of this Guide:

- 'An Introduction to Essay Writing in Psychology' (p. 17)
- Chapter 6, 'Finding and Using Resources'
- Follow the 11 steps for researching and writing essays (p. 50) and use the essay checklist (p. 53).

---

[1] It's worth noting that the APA Manual contains the complete rules for writing in the journals the APA publishes. The APA does not publish all the journals in Psychology. Other Psychology journals have different rules, so learn the reasons for the rules, rather than rigidly adhering to the prescriptions.

The ability to carry out and present the results of a laboratory exercise

Read the sections of this Guide:

- 'Report Writing Introduction' (p. 57)
- Chapter 6, 'Finding and Using Resources'.
- Follow the research report formula (p. 58) and use the research report checklist (p. 76).

A basic understanding of statistical techniques and the design of experimentation in psychological inquiry

- Read Chapter 2 of *Psychological science: An introduction.*
- Answer the multiple-choice questions on the Web page.
- Practise using the statistics with the resources in Chapter 7 of this Guide.
- If you have an examination, then read 'Sitting Examinations' (p. 146) in this Guide.

A broad knowledge of the theories and research that define Psychology as a subject matter

- Read *Psychological science: An introduction* completely.
- Take effective review notes from each chapter. See pages 107–8 of this Guide.
- Answer the short answer questions that accompany each chapter.
- Write short notes on each critical thinking issue raised in the chapters.
- Review your knowledge of each chapter by answering the multiple-choice questions on the Web page.
- Extend you revision by answering the questions posted on the Web page.
- Develop a revision schedule.
- Read 'Sitting Examinations' (p. 146) in this Guide.

CHAPTER 2
CAREERS IN PSYCHOLOGY

OVERVIEW

Introduction
2.1 Skills acquired in undergraduate Psychology
2.2 Clinical Psychology
2.3 Organisational Psychology
2.4 Academic Psychology
2.5 Counselling
2.6 Sports Psychology
2.7 Forensic Psychology
2.8 Educational and Developmental Psychology
2.9 Other uses for Psychology

INTRODUCTION

Psychology is a diverse discipline and the skills, knowledge and training one can acquire will reflect one's interest, background experience, educational commitment and career path. Your investment in studying Psychology will be repaid across your lifetime—this is almost guaranteed. The difficulty arises with the question of whether you will gain financially by studying Psychology. Some people study Psychology for interest only. Realistically, though, a lengthy investment in a course of study should achieve some practical benefit. Therefore, it is reasonable to ask the question 'What can I do with a degree in Psychology?'.

An interest in studying Introductory Psychology is often motivated from information gathered from the media, television, personal contacts and personal experiences. However, the true image of Psychology and its real value are distorted by the media and sometimes personal contacts can be narrow in the sort of advice they provide.

The most important point to recognise is that you are embarking on a course of study that will provide you with generalised and transferable skills. Psychology is almost unique because graduates acquire a blend of science and humanities skills, and a range of public and private sector agencies value this special mix. Some of those skills are learnt in developing essay writing skills, which, as you will find in Chapters 3, are a unique craft in Psychology. You will develop strategies and skills for handling complex information gathered by research scientists and be able to critically appraise that material, develop a perspective and present that information clearly to a considered audience.

■

Experience is a good teacher, but she sends in terrific bills.
Minna Antrim

2.1 Skills acquired in undergraduate Psychology

The skills you will acquire in completing an undergraduate degree in Psychology include:

1. Writing skills: expertise in formal writing, strategies for conveying complex information efficiently.
2. Reasoning: analytic sophistication.
3. Data analysis: an understanding and experience in the use of statistics and measurement.
4. Computer literacy: word-processing, data analysis, database development and communications.
5. Information access skills: literature and information searching.
6. Research skills: measurement, design and implementation of techniques to solve problems.
7. Pragmatism: a solution-oriented approach to complex problems that transfers to practical benefits.

These skills are important to keep in mind so that you do not focus too heavily on some vocational outputs that are traditionally associated with the study of Psychology. General skills are valuable and will reward you in whatever vocation you undertake.

Listed below is information about various careers. The order of the listing reflects the level of interest in each occupation. As a general piece of advice, it's a good idea to contact someone who is already working within the professional capacity that you wish to pursue. You may not have a clear idea about this until after you have completed your introductory course, or perhaps your degree, but do keep the idea in mind. The best advice comes from those with personal experience in the field you wish to enter. Most people will view a call inquiring about such things as part of their professional responsibilities, so they will generally give you some time to discuss their experience. Sometimes an e-mail will do the trick.

■

> Great work is done by people who are not afraid to be great.
> *Fernando Flores*

One tremendous difficulty outlining careers for psychologists is that different countries have different laws and different expectations of the types of training and appropriate qualifications for psychologists. You will need to develop an understanding of the particular requirements within your country and your career. One way to do this is to contact or join a society of professional psychologists. A wealth of advice is provided by specialist associations for psychologists, both for those beginning and those working in a career. There are three important associations for your purposes:

1. Australian Psychological Society: http://www.psychsociety.com.au/
2. New Zealand Psychological Society: http://www.psychology.org.nz/
3. American Psychological Association: http://www.apa.org

Each site is also listed on the Bond and McConkey Web page:
www.mcgraw-hill.com.au/mhhe/psychology/bond/

These sites offer a tremendous amount of information for professionals and students as they progress to choose their role within Psychology. Student memberships are possible within each organisation. Further to this, you will probably find some general advice from your careers centre at your university. These people will help you construct the elective courses you should be taking to advance along your chosen career path. They may even be Psychology graduates!

The term 'registered'

In New Zealand, the term 'registered psychologist' means something different from in Australia. In Australia, registration as a psychologist is governed by State or Territory Acts and there is some variation across the States and Territories in the requirements for registration. In New Zealand, the term 'registered psychologist' is governed by *The Psychologists Act* 1981. In New Zealand, it is possible for anyone to call themselves a psychologist but it is against the law to represent yourself as a registered psychologist unless you meet the requirements for registration, register and maintain the conditions of registration, which sometimes involves a practising certificate, supervision and professional standards of conduct. In practice, in New Zealand, the people who gain significant benefit from registering as psychologists are clinical psychologists. Academics, organisational psychologists, educational psychologists and psychologists in other specialities may not be registered and there is no legislative requirement to do so.

In Australia, the spirit of the legislation is the same but registration and its requirements applies to a broader range of occupations for psychologists. Generally, registration requires four full-time years of academic study in Psychology and two additional full-time years of post-graduate training or supervised experience. This experience requirement is broad enough to cover such things as human resource management. These differences in regulations and requirements for registration in turn reflect the types of training that people will engage with to achieve the requirements of their professional career.

■

He who can, does. He who cannot, teaches.
George Bernard Shaw

2.2 Clinical Psychology

2.2.1 Avoiding myths: some truths about clinical psychologists

- There are many more psychologists than clinical psychologists.
- Clinical psychologists are not psychiatrists, although they may work with them. Psychiatrists have a medical degree and specialised training in psychiatry. Psychiatry can be considered a speciality of medicine, much like that of a surgeon who specialises after completing a medical degree.
- A person with an undergraduate degree in Psychology is not necessarily even a psychologist but is certainly not a clinical psychologist.
- A counsellor is not a clinical psychologist, although a clinical psychologist may be a counsellor.
- You cannot do a one-year course in Psychology to be a clinical psychologist.

2.2.2 Career path for a clinical psychologist

Occasionally, people who complete a Master's degree or a PhD will return to study Clinical Psychology. In this case, those returning generally undertake the specialised Master's courses they may not have done when they did their postgraduate studies. Most people will gain entry into a course of study for

Clinical Psychology only *after* their first year of a Master's degree in Psychology. A few people may gain entry to a course of Clinical Psychology after their undergraduate degree. Almost certainly, the places in a course of Clinical Psychology will be extremely limited! A selection process will evaluate your past experience, suitability to be a clinical psychologist, academic ability and enthusiasm.

To gain experience, clinical psychologists generally work for some period in a hospital, community mental health service and psychiatric institution or as part of the criminal justice system. They may do their internship in such a setting.

2.2.3 Areas in which clinical psychologists work

A clinical psychologist may:

1. work within the justice system conducting rehabilitation programs for offenders, particularly sex offenders
2. work for the courts providing assessments and information to aid judges develop an understanding of the particulars of cases involving:
   (a) youth offending
   (b) guardianship and custodial issues
   (c) separation and divorce counselling
3. work in private practice aiding those who unable to work or have suffered emotional or mental injury
4. work with community health centres
5. provide services to or work within specialist agencies dealing with drug, alcohol and gambling addictions
6. specialise to become a clinical neuropsychologist to diagnose and assess brain injury and the effect of neurological impairment on cognitive functioning.

Not many people have the money to support seeing a clinical psychologist for personal problems they experience. Insurance companies, government agencies or businesses will fund most consultations with clinical psychologists.

2.3 Organisational Psychology

2.3.1 Avoiding myths

- Organisational psychologists do not make huge amounts of money but they do earn more than other psychologists on average. (See www.laseirra.edu/psychology/careers/careersi.htm for a bar graph outlining salaries of various psychologists. Note the information is derived from a US sample. See http://www.careers.co.nz/jobs/10b_bus/j80211e.htm for an understanding of and statistics on incomes for psychologists in this field in New Zealand.)

- Organisational psychologists do not only work in the corporate sector. Organisational Psychology owes its strength from the nurturing it gained as a discipline in the armed services. The army, navy and airforce are still leading employers of graduates.
- Human resource advisers are not organisational psychologists, although an organisational psychologist may be a human resource adviser.

2.3.2 Career path of an organisational psychologist

If you plan to become a specialised organisational psychologist, consider taking elective courses that have some relevance to the occupation, such as introductory law, management science, commercial law, computer science, accounting and economics.

2.3.3 Areas of speciality for organisational psychologists

An Organisational Psychologist may work in such areas of speciality as:

1. industrial relations
2. negotiation and mediation
3. training and career transfer
4. occupational health and safety
5. recruitment and selection, training, appraisal and review
6. vocational guidance and career development
7. ergonomics, job redesign
8. marketing.

The armed services

You will find further information on the armed services by contacting your local recruitment office. The armed services sometimes employ Psychology graduates with BA (Hons) or BSc (Hons) degrees and then assist with training to complete their specialisation in Organisational Psychology. The armed services require psychologists to undertake officer selection boards because all psychologists are commissioned officers.

2.4 Academic Psychology

2.4.1 Avoiding myths

- Not all academic psychologists are lecturers.
- Lecturers do not just lecture; they research, write, consult and review.

- Lecturers do not have a job with really good holiday entitlements.
- Lecturers do not generally repeat the same material in their lectures year after year.
- You do not need to be a genius to be a lecturer. Full Professors have failed subjects or done poorly through some part of their university careers. If you plan to be an academic psychologist, you will need to do reasonably well at Psychology. However, even famous people sometimes struggle. The classic genius, according to Ochse (1990), is a B+ student.

2.4.2 A normal career path for an academic psychologist

Nowadays, a completed PhD or its equivalent (DPsych, PsyD, DPhil) is often required to be a lecturer. However, people with Master's degrees often take up other sorts of jobs such as teaching fellowships, assistant lecturing and research fellowships while working towards PhDs. Academic psychologists invest an enormous amount of time into their training and then expend even more effort developing a speciality and expertise in an area in which they will research. Most psychologists will not reach their academic peak until they are in their fifties or sixties, unlike mathematicians, who generally succeed relatively early, typically before they are 30 years old.

2.5 Counselling

2.5.1 Avoiding myths

- Counsellors do not necessarily have any background in Psychology.
- Counsellors do not necessarily have a degree.
- In New Zealand and Australia, there are no laws preventing anyone calling themselves a counsellor or practising as a counsellor. There are associations of counsellors that recognise qualifications and oversee professional standards of conduct.
- Your own personal crises in life are not the experience you will need to be a good counsellor.
- No one is ever too old, or too young, to start training as a counsellor. However, the type of work a counsellor does may benefit from youth on the one hand (youth counsellors, school counsellors) and life experience on the other (marriage guidance, grief counselling).
- A clinical psychologist and a counsellor normally have very different training.

Although a counsellor may not have any background in Psychology, good counsellors should have some understanding of Psychology because they interact professionally with clinical psychologists, educational psychologists and perhaps even psychiatrists. Counsellors often develop experience in another vocation before becoming counsellors. The right sort of background experience that might lead to a career in counselling might include vocations such as teaching, social work, nursing and law, or experience as a religious leader, community worker or some other caring role.

Since many of the vocations listed above may develop out of an undergraduate degree in Psychology, it is worth recognising that these other careers are analogous to postgraduate training.

2.5.2 Areas of speciality for counsellors

Counsellors may end up working in the following sorts of careers:

- marriage and separation counselling
- organisational counselling: helping employees with problems related to life and career stress
- school counselling
- vocational counselling:
- health and welfare services
- private practice.

2.6 Sports Psychology

2.6.1 Avoiding myths

- Sports Psychology is not a new discipline.
- Sports Psychology draws on many areas of mainstream Psychology.

Sports Psychology has attracted an increasing and seemingly inexhaustible interest over recent years. Despite this, university Psychology departments rarely offer Sports Psychology courses. Certainly, if Sports Psychology is taught, it will often be within a Master's program alongside traditional specialities such as motivation, emotion, Social Psychology, and Biological and Physiological Psychology. It is by drawing on these areas of interest that sports psychologists gain the ability to assist sportspeople to do their best. A sports psychologist might develop strategies to assist athletes to maintain well-being, overcome anxiety, increase arousal levels, interact with others more effectively and deal with emotional stress.

The most important point to appreciate is that Sports Psychology would best be considered as a career option if your experience or intended training were augmented with some related field, such as sports medicine, occupational therapy or physiotherapy. Sports science is certainly an exciting and interesting field of development but it is by its nature multidisciplinary.

2.7 Forensic Psychology

2.7.1 Avoiding myths

- There are not enough serial killers to keep forensic psychologists employed full-time trying to track them down.
- The 'Silence of the Lambs' is not based on a true story.
- Forensic psychologists do not 'see' into the criminal mind.
- Forensic psychologists do not have special techniques for extracting confessions from criminals.
- Lie detectors, or the polygraph, may be used by forensic psychologists but are notoriously unreliable pieces of equipment. Lie detectors are not permissible as evidence in either the Australian or New Zealand courts.

In reality, forensic psychologists deal with far less interesting things than those that entertain us on television. A forensic psychologist is likely to have a background in Clinical Psychology but those psychologists with a background in law, sociology, criminology or social work may be usefully employed in the context of the criminal justice system.

2.7.2 Areas in which forensic psychologists work

- Forensic settings, such as prisons and rehabilitation clinics, for problems associated with criminal behaviour, such as anger management, alcohol and drug rehabilitation, and gambling and sexual offending behaviour modification.
- Providing psychological assessment.
- Researching issues concerning the criminal justice system and criminal offending.
- Training of police recruits.

Forensic psychologists also generally acquire some training within a Master's program. Unless the Psychology degree is combined with another degree, such as social work or law, or with extensive experience as a probation officer, police officer or prison officer, it is unlikely that an undergraduate degree would be sufficient to pursue this field. However, an undergraduate degree in Psychology may lead to a career in any of these related fields and that, when combined with experience and some future postgraduate study, may propel you into a career as a forensic psychologist.

2.8 Educational and Developmental Psychology

One of the most undervalued areas of Psychology is in the area of education. Developing a background in Psychology within an undergraduate degree, plus an additional background in counselling or teaching, would lead nicely to the vocational requirements of school guidance counsellors. With further training and experience, people can develop a professional role that uses a knowledge of Psychology as much as does any industrial or clinical psychologist. Despite this, not many people ask about this option and yet many people who study Psychology do not want to pursue the higher levels of study that are required for the professions described above.

There is scope to advance from this experience to more specialist professional roles. Government departments that oversee the education system seek out those who have an expertise in Developmental or Educational Psychology. In New Zealand, these departments are the Special Education Services, and the New Zealand Council for Educational Research.

Educational and Developmental Psychologists provide counselling services, assessment of aptitude and intelligence, advice on behaviour management, and a whole range of professional services to assist the management and development of the education system. It is a good option for people to consider; especially those who feel that neither Clinical nor Industrial Psychology are quite their things.

2.9 Other uses for Psychology

Psychologists can be found working in government departments as policy analysts, particularly in areas of health and education. Those departments that deal with traffic and occupational health and safety will employ psychologists to research and write reports. Psychologists with strong skills for analysing statistical information may be employed within some areas of medical research, especially those concerning public health, by analysing attitudes and behaviour concerning health issues, such as vaccinations, hygiene, use of medical resources and so on.

CHAPTER 3
ESSAY WRITING IN PSYCHOLOGY

OVERVIEW

3.1 An introduction to essay writing in Psychology
3.2 The essay formula
3.3 Refinements to the formula
3.4 Essay style
3.5 Things to avoid
3.6 Referencing
3.7 Essentials of the referencing formulae
3.8 Frequently asked questions
3.9 Ten easy steps for researching and writing essays
3.10 The essay checklist

3.1 An introduction to essay writing in Psychology

3.1.1 Why do we write essays?

It is inevitable that you will be asked to write essays and yet few academic psychologists ever write essays for publication. Philosophers write essays. Psychologists generally write research reports, review articles, books and commentaries. The books or journals you are referred to will seldom contain anything that even resembles an essay, certainly not a 1500 word essay. An article in *Scientific American* about an area of Psychology will be close to an essay. The commentaries that occasionally appear in *Psychological Review* are very good essays. Still, no one will really expect you to read these at the introductory level. Why are you asked to write essays? This is largely because some of the components of research reports, review articles and books are similar to essays. Ultimately, you are asked to write essays because the skills involved in an essay's production transfer to all our other types of writing.

3.1.2 Other subjects approach essay writing differently

You may be taking subjects that fit alongside Psychology, such as sociology, philosophy, biology and law, or perhaps you are taking English. Each subject's department will probably give you a guide to writing essays as there are lessons from every discipline about structure, writing and argument. However, Psychology has a curious blend of science and arts which makes it different when it comes to essay writing. A guide to writing an essay in philosophy or English will let you down on the science side of things. A guide in biology may let you down on the way to structure your argument and critically appraise theory.

Your Psychology department will probably also give you an essay writing guide. You will normally be given a guide on how to reference the works you cite as Psychology has a unique method of referencing. If not, there is a short guide to referencing below. You must read the Psychology guide to essay writing no matter how able you are in other subjects: a sociological or philosophical essay is unlikely to score particularly well in Introductory Psychology.

The aim below is to cut across the formality of essay writing guides and get to the practical issue—how you can focus your effort and maximise your output when writing essays. That is, the mechanics of writing a Psychology essay, as opposed to any other sort of writing, that are dealt with here.[2] Some hints and practical advice are offered to help you develop your writing, or at least unravel some of the mysteries behind essay writing, and provide you with successful strategies for getting good grades.

3.1.3 An analogy about essay writing in Psychology

Philosophers are considered the experts at writing essays; it's a necessary aspect of their subject material. However, take the example of a philosophical writer who never really wrote any essays and yet was extremely successful. Ludwig Wittgenstein (1889–1951) was regarded as poorly read, rarely referenced the work of others and wrote in an almost impenetrable dialectic[3] between himself

---

[2] How to argue and where to get resources from are dealt with in separate sections of this Guide. You should consider reading the material about developing an argument (pp. 84–87) before you launch too far into writing your essay—especially if you're a bit stuck on your argument.

[3] An argumentative exchange.

and an interlocutor.[4] He wrote without introductions or conclusions (he simply ends), and he wrote without the formal structure of conjoining paragraphs or chapters. Ironically, he wrote about language and logic. It seems unimaginable that a philosopher could succeed without becoming an expert essay writer. What was his approach?[5]

Wittgenstein enjoyed reading comic books about detectives and crime stories and he likened his philosophical approach to that of a detective unravelling mysteries by gathering clues. Wittgenstein would write pieces of an argument in short paragraphs, sometimes even two line statements, and collected these into broader arguments (like a comic book but without pictures). Each piece served to build the whole of his argument. Each piece was one or other clue to a mystery that he would reveal in bigger arguments read as a whole. Wittgenstein succeeded with an approach to writing that would certainly be rejected in the modern context because he was extremely good at utilising this detective-like approach— Wittgenstein's arguments are frighteningly sophisticated and very important.

The point to be taken from Wittgenstein's approach is not that you can write an essay without an introduction or conclusion, use two line paragraphs or read comic books to become a famous philosopher. You will certainly fail Psychology by adopting any of these approaches.[6] The point is that an argument is the most essential feature of writing an essay, at least in philosophy. However, the detective analogy has a greater application in Psychology. The types of evidence we have for building our arguments are more diverse and important than they are in philosophy. Consequently, the detective approach is a good one. Your task in researching, arguing and writing an essay is like gathering the evidence of a crime, evaluating how it was done, developing a case for who the perpetrator was, and presenting that case to a judge. This analogy will be used throughout this chapter.

To extend the analogy, there are rules of the court. You must present your case with as much rigmarole as accompanies a court trial. You must reference your work properly, use formal English, adopt the correct structure, define your concepts and get the right evidence in the right order, lest you be challenged by an opponent (the marker). Your essay is an argument. You are trying to convince your reader (the judge) of a viewpoint you have developed on a particular set of issues (the case). From this perspective the essay task might seem more appealing. You might recognise that you are doing a greater range of tasks than a typical lawyer might do—you can point this out to your law school contemporaries but

---

[4] An imaginary person whom one argues against, who sometimes raises questions.

[5] If you treat the rhetorical question as if an imaginary person had asked it, then you've got the idea of an interlocutor. Don't use this technique in Psychology; it belongs to philosophy.

[6] See Heaton & Groves (1994) for a comic book about Wittgenstein that you might like to read.

be prepared to back up the statement with an argument.[7] You may still find the idea a bit daunting. The following guide will help prepare you.

3.2 The essay formula

Experienced students will claim that essay writing is easy once you get the knack of it. Nothing will replace actual experience. It is also sometimes suggested by experienced students that there is a formula for writing essays. They may cynically add that the formula constrains creativity and makes a banality of the whole process of essay writing. Banal or not, there is a loose formula for writing essays and your first task is to understand its structure.

Below is a typical question that might arise as an essay question in an Introductory Psychology course. Your essay question might be accompanied by a few hints and suggestions, plus a reading list that addresses a typically fairly general issue that you are asked to examine.

> **Example essay question:** 'Contrast the way Spearman and Gardner approached the study of intelligence.'

This question is fairly specific so as to show you the utility of the formula. Suppose the essay is to be 1500 words. That gives you 14–18 fairly short paragraphs. You are going to use two paragraphs before you start: one for an introduction and one for a conclusion.

3.2.1 An outline of the essay formula

Figure 3.1 provides an outline of the essay formula. The formula should be easy enough to follow. It is set out as a plan of how to tackle the question with some suggestions as to the content for each particular paragraph. In the right-hand column there is an indication of the order of writing. It's a mistake to think you start an essay at the first paragraph and work your way through to the end. Always start with the definitions of the key concepts in the essay question, then write the issue, then explain what you are going to write within a 'signposting' paragraph. After that, follow what you said you will do in that signposting section.

Of course, different questions will involve entirely different content and will require that you adjust the formula to accommodate your essay's particular

---

[7]   The argument relies on that fact that you'll learn to define what the evidence is, find the evidence and gather the evidence into a corpus of knowledge. Lawyers are typically told the material facts. You are both the expert witness and the one arguing the case. A lawyer may one day rely on the skills you develop in your studies. Go easy though, you may one day rely on a lawyer.

	Cover page	
	• Title	
	• Student details	
	Introduction	
Paragraph 1	Opening statement(s)	11
	• Something historical, topical or interesting about the content.	
	• Perhaps a quote from Spearman, or Gardner, or both.	
	• The point is to capture the reader.	
Paragraph 2	Historical context	12
	• Describe when Spearman and Gardner worked and their historical influences.	
	• A current context is equally useful here. Why is what went before important now?	
Paragraph 3	Concept definition	1
	• What do we mean by the term 'intelligence'?	
	• Definition from broad source (e.g. Corsini's *Encyclopedia of psychology* or Harré and Lamb's *The encyclopedic dictionary of psychology*).	
Paragraph 3	Signposting	3
	• State what you are going to discuss, in what order, and indicate what conclusion you will come to.	
	Main body of your essay	
Paragraph 4	The crux of the issue	2
	• Spearman and Gardner differed in their definitions of intelligence (you know they differed on something before you started, or else the question would not make any sense—normally the issue is the essay question).	
	• The purpose of this paragraph is to *state what the problem is*!	
	• What are the important differences in Spearman's and Gardner's approach to the study of intelligence?	
Paragraphs 5–6	Describe Spearman's approach	4
	• Outline Spearman's perspective on intelligence.	
	• Reference Spearman's (1927) *The abilities of man: Their nature and measurement*, and other notable works.	
Paragraphs 7–8	Describe Gardner's approach	5
	• What was the perceived difficulty with Spearman's approach or traditional approaches that are associated to Spearman?	
	• How did Gardner approach the problem? What solution did he propose?	
	• Mention the notable work: Gardner's (1983) *Frames of mind: The theory of multiple intelligences*.	

Fig. 3.1 An outline of the essay formula for the essay question 'Contrast the way Spearman and Gardner approached the study of intelligence'

	Main body of your essay (continued)	
Paragraphs 9–10	Evaluation • What are the advantages of each approach? • Is one better than the other? • Do they explain different things? • What problems develop from the differences?	7
Paragraphs 11–12	The experts • What do the experts say? • Other researchers and authors have approached the questions you confront. How did they deal with the issue? • What is the considered opinion?	6
Paragraph 13	Applications • Why would any of this matter? • What consequences are there in approaching the topic of intelligence from these contrasting positions? • Does this knowledge impact on everyday life? • Could things change because of this knowledge you have described?	8
	Conclusions	
Paragraph 14	Your input: narrow conclusions • You will have evaluated the material throughout and now is your opportunity to summarise the perspective you have adopted or extend your comments by detailing your perspective.	9
Paragraph 15	Conclusion: broad conclusions • Restate the issue, the crucial points of difference between Spearman and Gardner, what the experts say, and the consequences of it all.	10
	References	13
	How many references should there be? • Look through the formula: There is one for the quote, one for a definition, at least two for the notable works, a couple more for the experts and probably one or two for the applications: 7–8 minimum, but probably more.	

Fig. 3.1 An outline of the essay formula for the essay question 'Contrast the way Spearman and Gardner approached the study of intelligence' *(continued)*

emphasis. However, the components of an essay will not substantially alter with the question. You will always have definitions, signposting, conclusions and most of the other sections listed in bold in the middle column of Figure 3.1. If your question is really very different from this one, then at least consider writing out a plan that looks similar to the one presented in Figure 3.1.

In summary, the crucial elements of the formula given in Figure 3.1 are:

- introduction
- definitions
- signposting
- main body of the essay
- conclusions
- references.

■

Perfection is achieved, not when there is nothing more to add, but when there is nothing left to take away.

Antoine de Saint Exupery

3.2.2 Two cautions about using a formula

The formula is meant to help you but there are a couple of traps that need to be considered. The first is a consequence of this Guide. If you and everyone else in your class use it and write a formula essay, then it is likely that the best you can achieve is a slightly above average grade depending on how well you write the piece. Examiners give good grades to those essays that stand out as special in some significant way. Examiners give bad grades to those that fail to have the components of the formula or lack the fundamentals, such as paragraph construction and correct referencing. Sometimes examiners say that they evaluate essays according to objective standards. If this were true, then the formula essay would probably succeed in getting you a B to A grade. In practice, when a marker has seen numerous versions of the same essay, he or she will start to be less forgiving of any errors than if each essay has a unique structure. Examiners may also disagree with this formula. The formula above is broad enough to result in different essays for each application: it does work and with more experience it becomes second nature to apply it flexibly.

The more important second trap concerns what you input into the formula. You are likely to possess the same reading list, textbook and same sources of definitions that everyone else has. Imagine how the examiner feels when he or she reads Harré and Lamb's definition of intelligence for the twentieth time (there's nothing wrong with the definition, it just wears them down to see it often, and you are trying to hold their attention).

Also, it is an error to repeat sections from your textbook or follow its treatment of a topic area as if it provides the formula for your essay plan. There are two reasons for this. First, everyone else has the same information presented in the same order. Second, textbook chapters only look like essays—they start with definitions and end with summaries—but a textbook chapter is *not* an essay. A textbook chapter will generally lack the argument that you want to develop. A textbook chapter provides all the evidence but leaves you with the task of developing *your* case. You may use your textbook to gain a perspective on the argument. You should use your textbook as a source of basic evidence and clues to further information worth investigating. However, a textbook will not lead you to a conclusion, and the conclusion, like a lawyer's closing statement, is the most influential component of your performance.

Now, given these two problems, you are going to need to be creative. The solution is fairly obvious: find unique input, get unique output.[8]

■

Never express yourself more clearly than you think.

Niels Bohr

3.3 Refinements to the formula

3.3.1 Concept definitions

Harré and Lamb's *The encyclopedic dictionary of psychology* (1983) is a good source of definitions of concepts but it's not the only source. It's not the best source either. A good textbook that deals exclusively with the topic of interest will provide a better definition of the concept of interest. The principal reason for this is that a textbook will give more than one definition and provide a more detailed discussion of conceptual issues. Get a textbook and look for the definitions. You don't need to read the entire text. Most of what it contains will be beyond what you need, your interest and especially your time. Definitions appear in textbooks, as in essays and textbook chapters, at the beginning—the formula is applied elsewhere.

Find a few definitions and develop your 'concept definition' paragraph into an evaluation of these definitions. An evaluation might consider the overall theoretical perspective that seems to underlie all the definitions you find; or you might point out that different theoretical perspectives lead to different definitions. A behaviourist definition of 'learning', for example, will be very different from a definition proposed from a cognitive or information-processing perspective. (For a good example of this, look at the definitions developed at the beginning of Chapter 8 of Bond & McConkey, 2000, pp. P4.3–P4.4).

---

[8] A two line paragraph has been used here for emphasis—that's the short paragraph's function. Don't ever use it for any other reason and never write any section of an essay with a series of them. Business people often do this but it's wrong in formal writing

Never use an English dictionary to provide a definition. If you resort to this, you are wasting your potential grade for what is very little effort. It should take less than 20 minutes in a library to find a specialised text on the topic of your essay, find the section that deals with definitions and copy out the book's reference (remember the page number, you will need it). You are now secure in the knowledge that you know what you are writing about because you have examined the special terms in the essay question.

You may use a dictionary of Psychology for terms that are not likely to have a specialised text. Concepts developed by theorists fall into this category. You are unlikely to find a book that deals exclusively with Freud's concept of 'id' (though you may find a general text on Freud that defines it well). You may not be able to find a text that deals well with 'object permanence' or 'conservation', but again you will find a general text on Piaget and cognitive development that will define these. If the concept is a psychological concept but you think it is not important enough to find a text to research the concept, then a dictionary of Psychology will be the next best thing. You can also use the World Wide Web: this link is to a specialised dictionary on cognitive science: http://matrix.psych.ualberta.ca/~mike/Pearl_Street/Dictionary/search.html

The grading you will receive based on your definition source is shown in the table below.

Definition source	Grading
No definitions	D
Dictionary definitions	C
Psychology dictionary definitions	B/A
Definitions drawn from texts and original sources with some evaluation	A/A+

3.3.2 Signposting

Signposting is the technique of explaining to your reader where you are going with your argument. Signposts may be a series of statements that explain what you intend to argue, what evidence you will consider and what conclusion you intend to reach. Signposting provides the structure for your essay. When you receive comments such as 'lacks structure', you can be sure it is because you have not used any signposting. Signposts can be used throughout an essay and at the beginning and end of paragraphs.

An example of a type of signposting used in this chapter is the detective analogy; it acts as a reference point that you are familiar with. You may be hazy on essay writing but you have an idea of crimes, evidence and lawyers in court. This is popular knowledge so you have some idea of where we are heading when legal references are made because you will frame those references in terms of the detective solving a crime and presentation of the case to a judge. Analogies are sophisticated signposts and are not always appropriate for formal writing—you are unlikely to use them when you start out but keep the idea in mind for later. Signposting is like the opening statements of lawyers exclaiming how they will prove the accused is guilty or innocent—the point of signposts is to help structure the writing.

Here is some signposting taken from a review article by McClelland, McNaughton and O'Reilly (1995). Some text has been cut so that you can see the signposting in action, and the important parts are underlined:

> We begin with a brief overview of the neuropsychology of memory ... and elaborate one possible account of the functional organisation of memory that is broadly consistent with the neuropsychological evidence ... We then describe results from connectionist modelling research ... From the insight gained through the consideration of these models, we develop ... We discuss the implications of our view of the role of consolidation ... and we conclude with a comparison of our views with those of other ... (pp. 419–20).

Consider the fact that the quotation represents one paragraph, the third paragraph, of a 10 000 word article. If you compare its contents to the essay formula, you will see the order of the formula being represented to the reader. This is the way you should signpost. The only warning attaches to the use of the pronoun 'we'. You can use the personal pronoun 'I' in your signposting section but not elsewhere. It's best to avoid the use of personal pronouns entirely (see p. 37).

The point of signposting is to ease the burden on the reader, not for you to organise your argument. Have your essay well planned before you write your signposting and make sure you accomplish what your signposting suggests. If you change tack midway through your essay, you might offer another signpost at the end of the section just prior to the shift. Often this is done by saying something like 'The issue of whether intelligence is anything more than what intelligence tests measure is examined in the next section'. As you can see, the formula only serves as a base and should not be relied on too heavily. The grading you will receive based on your use of signposting is shown in the table below.

Signposting use	Grading
No signposting	D
Signposting within a single introductory paragraph	C
Signposting throughout	B/A
Sophisticated use of signposts throughout	A+

Note: If you don't follow your signposts, you will run into trouble with your grade. The outline here assumes that you actually do what you say you are going to do.

3.3.3 The crux of the issue

The crux of the issue is established early on in any piece of writing. You may have a great argument. You may have set out a wonderful signposting section explaining what you are going to do and even what conclusion you are going to reach. But the reader of an essay or article wants to know *why* you have put in the effort to research and write the essay. This part is easy for you. The motivation for the essay is not that you want to pass Introductory Psychology; it's the essay question you have been given.

Essay questions sometimes disguise the 'real' issue but you will soon uncover this in your reading and especially once you have examined the definitions (see pp. 92–3). Before you set about describing aspects of research and presenting the main body of your essay, you need to state the point of controversy, the importance of different approaches, or the most essential problem that psychologists are trying to understand. Whereas opening statements are meant to be creative to capture the reader's interest, in the crux of the issue you will write the issue and why it is important seriously, even at the risk of being boring.

Here is an example. Again, some of the content has been cut and the important parts underlined:

> Both the likelihood and simplicity principles explain, at least at an intuitive level a wide range of phenomena of perceptual organisation. <u>Consider, for example, the Gestalt law of good continuation,</u> that perceptual interpretations that involve continuous lines or contours are favoured. <u>The likelihood explanation is based</u> on the observation that continuous lines and contours are very frequent in the environment (e.g. <u>Brunswick, 1956</u>) ... <u>The simplicity explanation, by contrast,</u> suggests that continuous lines or contours are imposed on the stimulus when they allow the stimulus to be described more simply. (Chater, 1996, p. 566)

This is the fourth paragraph of another 10 000 word article. Again, the outline in the formula is used. The author has already defined the key components in the second paragraph, and outlined the signposting in the third paragraph. Now the author describes the controversy. The points to note are that the author describes both sides of a debate, uses an example to illustrate how these opposing views differ, and cites an example of a key proponent of one of those views.

Thus, you need to examine your question carefully and consider two things: who is involved in the debate and what is the issue? The people may be a group aligned theoretically (e.g. behaviourists) or they may be individuals—be aware that there may be more than two sides. The issue cannot be predicted but it will undoubtedly be revealed to you in your essay question. The difficult task is to write the section concisely and effectively. One way to do this is to choose an example and show how different perspectives approach the issues, as Chater (1996) has done in the example given. The minimal requirement is to paraphrase the question of your essay, but you can do better by introducing an example and citing one or two key references. The grading you will receive for your presentation of the crux of the issue is shown in the table below.

Crux of the issue presentation	Grading
No crux of the issue paragraph	D
Restating the question	C
Restating the question, providing an outline of how different perspectives approach the topic	B/A
Describe the issue, give an example of its relevance, provide an outline of how different perspectives approach the topic that relates to the example	A+

3.3.4 Evidence and in-text referencing

What counts as evidence for your argument is typically constrained by the question. An essay question usually is not controversial in a way that will allow you to produce a novel argument; it's normally a novel arrangement of facts within an argument that gains a good grade. Whoever sets the essay question will know of a debate in Psychology that has two or more sides that battle it out. Your task is to discover the debate, find the evidence, take a perspective on that evidence and represent your position coherently. Describing, evaluating and presenting the evidence is the main task of your essay; it's the main body of your essay and comprises what the formula states as 'describe', 'evaluation', 'the experts' and 'applications'.

You need to provide good, credible evidence for your argument. The research reported in books and journals is the evidence for your case. Describing a body of research involves presenting the research that has led to our understanding of the issue to this point. Evaluating the evidence involves presenting the similarities among research findings and presenting the differences. A lawyer may present facts such as: 'his fingerprints were on the gun'; 'he was standing over the body when the police arrived and the witness saw him go into the building with the victim'. You will present facts such as: 'H. M.[9] suffered from anterograde amnesia'; 'H. M. could still learn practical tasks but had no memory of performing those tasks'; 'H. M. had the hippocampal region removed by surgery; thus the hippocampal region of the brain has something to do memory and there is a need to divide memory into different types of ability (implicit and explicit memory)'.

Because you are not coming up with the evidence by doing the actual research, your task is to frame the evidence in your argument so you will need to rely on others to provide the evidence for your case. Most of what goes into your essay will come from readings, texts and research papers (see p. 97). It is this requirement that makes the notion of referencing so crucial.

---

[9] You can read about H. M. in Bond and McConkey (2000, Chapter 10).

Notice the way textbooks are replete with citations to studies. Textbooks are the collection of evidence that constitutes a subject matter—they are a great source of evidence. The textbook is *not* the evidence itself; it merely reports the evidence. So, by simple reasoning, you know not to cite your textbook, although there are exceptions to the rule (e.g. for definitions). Also, try to avoid referring to newspapers as providing evidence as they rarely do. Newspaper articles report research; they do not present it for scrutiny.

As you will note in the essay formula, about six to seven references are required for any essay. You don't get credit for having a long reference list. It's not how many references you cite and it's not necessarily what you cite, but how you use your citations that is really the important issue.

3.3.4.1 In-text referencing

Leaving aside referencing in the section at the end called 'references' (never a bibliography), you have the task of putting some references into the body of your essay. Referencing the works of others will avoid any suggestion that you have copied the works of others or what is known as plagiarism (see below).[10] However, the primary reason for referencing is that the work of others is your evidence. Good use of referencing is the way to really hone your grade. Good students reference well. They are not necessarily reading any more than students who score poorly, but good use of referencing techniques organises an argument in such a way to provide it with clarity and precision and brings out the writer's argument—your argument.

Without a reference the claim you make may come across like 'the accused is innocent because someone saw him in the bar at the time of the crime'. The Prosecutor says 'who?' and the defence cannot produce the witness. No one should believe the claim, even if it is true! The witness has to appear. You must produce your witnesses too and the way to do so is to reference your claims. To be credible evidence, your claims need to be fully acknowledged so that they can be scrutinised for accuracy by your reader—almost like the other lawyer having the right to cross-examine the witness you call.

3.3.4.2 Examples of in-text referencing

The following examples of in-text referencing are drawn from Walton and Bathurst (1998). The study concerned the research finding that most drivers consider themselves better-than-average drivers, which of course is logically impossible, and it's 'no *mean* feat' (Alicke, Klotz, Breitenbecher, Yurak, & Vredenburg, 1995). While it seems humorous that we are all likely to say we are better-than-average drivers, the bias has serious implications for safety campaigns. Researchers have labelled this bias 'the self-enhancement bias'.

---

[10] You shouldn't even need to consider the issue if you follow the rest of this Guide.

The types of in-text referencing can be organised into four broad types: citing as evidence, listing as evidence, pointing, and quoting. You may reference for other reasons. You know already that citing definitions, for example, is a special case when you would use an in-text reference. Still, these techniques should provide an adequate base for you to get the essential types of referencing.

3.3.4.3 Citing research as evidence

When presenting your evidence, start with the general case. You want to start with the broadest study you can find. Often this is very clear in the material you read because everyone else will report that study as central to the research program. For example:

> Svenson (1981), for example, found that between 70–90% of drivers, in his sample, claimed to be safer and more skilful than the average driver.

The short statement outlines the essential feature of Svenson's study. The study found that people demonstrate a biased perception of their skill and safety as drivers. Note that you only need a short statement to describe the research. There is no need to describe the whole study, where it was completed and so on unless the study is very important or such a discussion is demanded by the argument you are developing.

When developing your description of the evidence of a particular area, expand into more detail. When another study has an element that makes its evidence more particular than the general case, then you might write it like this:

> People claim to be more considerate, reliable, wise and responsible (McCormick, Walkey & Green, 1986) although the bias was eliminated when the reference was to a 'very good driver' rather than the 'average driver'.

The study by McCormick et al. (1986) expands the finding of the bias into other areas and introduces a twist because it has an added dimension that Svenson didn't investigate. This was the crucial point that Walton and Bathurst (1998) wanted to examine. However, all the reference does here is to point out the 'facts' stating that these findings were produced.

From these examples you may gain a sense in which your argument develops by treating research findings as pieces of evidence for a broader case. Whatever else you take away from this Guide, learn that research is evidence and that your skill in presenting research to support your argument and build your case is fundamental. Referencing cleverly is the way to build the best arguments.

3.3.4.4 Listing research as evidence

Often it is useful to list a whole lot of research as evidence of the case you are developing. You can make the point you want to say and simply add in the relevant studies as evidence of that general point.

The effect has been found in Sweden, the United States (Svenson, 1981, 1985), France (Delhomme, 1991) and New Zealand (McCormick et al. 1986).

Alternatively, from Chapter 15 in your textbook:

The question has been most vigorously argued by Lazarus (e.g. 1982, 1984, 1991, 1993).

The first list simply indicates that the authors are aware that studies have been performed in other countries (it's not even a complete list). You can do this with almost any series of studies once you write out the point that is crucial to your argument. Alternatively, you can reason from the list to the point you want to make. Here, the issue is the reliability of the self-enhancement bias. Since the finding has been repeated across several cultures, we can be convinced that it is not a peculiar finding of one sample of drivers. The second example states that the authors are aware of a point being defended on a number of occasions and the list of citations from the one author indicates the endurance of that argument.

3.3.4.5 *Pointing*

'Pointing' is the technique of stating that you are aware of a broader discussion without dealing with that issue in your essay. Many students get bogged down in material because they do not adequately grasp the notion of pointing, think they are cheating because they may have limited knowledge of the things they point to, or feel they want to include everything that impacts on the case they are developing. All these anxieties are unnecessary. When you have a word limit, pointing to studies by skilful referencing is the most essential technique to grasp (which is one reason lecturers and tutors talk about getting referencing right).

Studies of drivers' attitudes towards their safety and skill have revealed a seemingly universal phenomenon of self-enhancement bias (Delhomme, 1991).

Why Delhomme (1991)? Because Delhomme (1991) claims that the phenomenon of driver overconfidence transcends cultures. Delhomme's study is about a range of other things so the reference only points to one particular feature of Delhomme's discussion. Walton and Bathurst (1998) didn't want to discuss whether the bias was universal, the underlying theory as to why it should be devoid of cultural content and so on, so they pointed to Delhomme (1991), who provides an expanded discussion on the subject. Referencing this way gives you credit for researching the issue, focusing your discussion and keeping your writing concise. Most importantly, pointing allows you to dedicate your argument to a limited range of important elements without seeming to narrow your focus and avoid discussing relevant material.

Think about pointing as giving directions or an instruction on where something is located. When someone asks you where he or she left his/her car keys and you point and say 'over there', you give the least but sufficient clue to assist that person. The same applies to your referencing of something not quite central to your concerns but of sufficient concern that others might think it is an important issue and need your help in navigating through issues.

3.3.4.6 *Quotations*

Quotations are very different from citations although they function similarly to the other in-text referencing techniques described above. A quotation states exactly what another author has written. Quotations go in quotation marks and are referenced with a page number. You cannot point to a quotation nor list quotations. A series of quotations run together is almost meaningless in the context of your essay. You should find yourself using quotations sparingly. Never run a series of quotations together. Students often do this to avoid the accusation of plagiarism but this is a poor strategy.

When you think about quotations as evidence for the case you are developing, you will soon realise that they are very different to citations of research. A quotation is something someone says about research or an argument he/she presents. What that person or persons say may be well reasoned or misinformed. Just because someone has written something down doesn't make it evidence of anything other than that particular person's thinking about a set of issues or research. Thus, you know that when you are quoting you are not presenting evidence about research; you are presenting someone else's view of that research or evidence.

A very good rule of thumb is used in philosophy: *only quote what you disagree with*. The rule doesn't apply to opening statements and concept definitions. When students develop a habit of quoting large chunks of material, they tend to do so without evaluating what they quote. In terms of the legal analogy, it comes across to your audience like 'Well, he must be innocent because Skinner said so!' or 'And, look here he said it again, and someone else agreed with him'. If you quote (not cite) only what you disagree with, you will be forced to state the point of disagreement. Then it comes across like 'My learned friend suggests to you that it was done with a candlestick but there was no evidence of any blood stains and the accumulation of dust indicates the object hadn't been moved for some time'. Note that you would *quote* the 'learned friend', *cite* the evidence of the 'accumulation of dust' and *point* to the 'lack of evidence' of bloodstains. This approach will give you credit for critical thinking and help you develop original lines of argument. The additional advantage is that you will look for points of disagreement when you read material.

> This methodological ambiguity led Groeger and Grande (1996) to criticise, correctly, McKenna et al. (1991) for their assumption that their results are, 'more consistent with a self enhancement bias rather than a downward comparison theory' (p. 50).

Walton and Bathurst (1998) went on to outline their disagreement with McKenna et al. (1991) and so the quotation defines the point on which they disagreed with McKenna et al. (1991) and they have pointed to another discussion in Groeger and Grande (1996).

3.3.4.7 Rules for in-text referencing

There are technical rules for how citations should appear in the text of your essay, as well as at the end. Where to put the page reference is a judgment call. The above example might have put 'McKenna et al. (1991, p. 50) for their assumption that their results are "more consistent ..." ' instead of placing the page reference after the completion of the quotation. How many authors you list out depends on the number of authors. It's listed as McKenna et al. (the 'et al.' means 'and others') to avoid having to write McKenna, Stanier and Lewis (1991) all the time. When you cite a list of researchers, repeating all the authors becomes clumsy after a while. The first time you cite a multiple-authored citation you write out all the authors, while the second time you can use the abbreviation 'et al.' (see Table 3.1 for further details).

When the quotation runs over two or more pages of the text you are quoting, the 'p. 50' becomes, for example, 'pp. 50–51'. A quotation that runs for more than 40 words is called a block quotation and should be indented without quotation marks as shown in this text. If you insert words into a quotation, you put square brackets around them [like this], and if you omit material, you put ellipsis points ('...').

3.3.4.8 Some technical rules for citations

Table 3.1 lists some technical rules for in-text referencing.

Table 3.1 Technical rules for citations

Authors	First use of the reference	Second use of the reference	Variation
1	Harré (1989) argues ...	Harré (1989) argues ...	... this conclusion (Harré, 1989)
2	Taylor and Brown (1989) conjecture ...	Taylor and Brown (1989) conjecture ...	... has been offered (Taylor & Brown, 1989).
3–5	McKenna, Stanier and Lewis (1991) found ...	McKenna et al. (1991) found ...	... the finding (McKenna et al., 1991).
6+	Skutella, Criswell, Moy, Probst, Breese, Jirikowski, Holsboer (1994) investigated ...	Skutella, Criswell, et al. (1994) investigated ...	... in their investigation (Skutella, Criswell, et al., 1994).
Same author, but multiple reference in the same year of publication Use lower case letters to distinguish the papers			Harré (1989a), Harré (1989b)
Same author, but multiple references in different years Separate the years with a semicolon			Jones (1985; 1986; 1990)

3.3.4.9 Most frequently asked question

'What if I haven't read the actual reference that I want to cite?'

You may find a text that examines material that you want to cite as evidence. Suppose you find in Bond and McConkey (2000) a section that deals with a series of articles and you want to cite the studies because the text's discussion of the article is sufficient for your purposes. Let's assume you haven't read any of the articles that Bond and McConkey (2000) refer to. Whom do you cite? Sometimes people will cite such things as: '(Schacter & Singer, 1962 as cited in Bond & McConkey, 2000)'. This is one way to reference something you haven't read, but it's clumsy. Honesty is the best policy. You can say it like this:

> Bond and McConkey (2000) treat Schacter and Singer (1962) as providing the evidence that cognitive and social factors interpret undifferentiated arousal as an emotional state.

Now, you haven't stated anything illegitimate with your claim. When you are talking about more than one article and wanting to 'list research as evidence' this approach is best. You can say:

> Bond and McConkey (2000) present five studies that deal with the issue of intelligence testing in schools (Jones, 1978; Fisher, 1967; Cormick, 1987; Pilcher & Brown, 1991; Vernon, 1994). These studies are thought to provide evidence that intelligence testing provides an accurate assessment of school-aged children's future ability to perform scholastically.

This approach avoids the essay containing numerous 'as cited in' references that show that you haven't read beyond your text, which is not the impression you want to give. Texts such as Bond and McConkey (2000) are useful reading that you should exploit fully, so don't avoid citing their references—just do so cleverly.

Referencing correctly will allow you to develop your argument or the perspective you want to adopt on the material at hand. You might enter a longer discussion as to the adequacy of the research design adopted by the researchers you have looked at and pointed to. You might identify areas of research that haven't been performed or you think should be performed. You might simply develop a discussion of the usefulness of the information that researchers have obtained. For other suggestions on developing an argument see page 84. The grading you will receive for your use of in-text referencing is shown in the table below.

In-text referencing	Grading
No references	D
Referencing limited to direct quotations	C
Citing research as evidence	B/A
Citing research as evidence, listing research as evidence, pointing and quoting	A/A+

Note: Your grading for referencing isn't entirely dependent on the number of references or type of referencing you adopt; there is also the quality and the completeness of your references. Again, a good text and your reading list are the key to obtaining an overview of the relevant material.

3.3.5 Opening statements and historical context

Opening statements

The essay formula allows some creativity with opening statements. Your essay grade will have no formal marking allocation set against your opening sentence and yet this sentence is probably the most influential on the marker. The best opening statements draw in the reader by hitting them with something topical, controversial or historically interesting. You will find material for your opening statement in literature, the media, in the issues in your community, culture or activities. Good opening lines often involve issues that appear in newspapers, government reports or statements made by people, especially when the remarks are enduring enough to be referenced.

Never write an opening sentence such as 'In this essay I shall examine the …' or rephrase the essay question as 'The issue of whether …' or 'In contrasting Spearman's and Gardner's approach …'. If you feel the need to do this, then the place to do this is in the crux of the issue section.

It is sometimes suggested that clichés and rhetorical questions should be avoided in all parts of formal writing. Perhaps they should but they can be used to good effect in an opening statement. Never use rhetorical questions and clichés anywhere else in your essay. You can use a rhetorical question but be careful not to be too emotive because it may come across as 'Isn't it possible the butler did it?', which is just too lame. Here are a few examples of opening statements:

> In attempting to change stereotypes, people often point to famous exceptions. If Margaret Thatcher could rule Britain with an iron fist, surely women are capable of being tough leaders. (Kunda & Oleson, 1997, p. 965)

Note that 'iron fist' is a cliché and the expression 'surely women are capable of being tough leaders' is a rhetorical question.

> Human beings are constantly faced with the need to reason, to infer something novel from available information. If John's friend tells him that she will be either at home or at work and he cannot reach her at work, John fully expects her to pick up the phone when he calls her house (Polk & Newell, 1995).

The use of an example, even a hypothetical one, can be used to hit the reader with the point of the study. The study here concerns how people, like John, combine two pieces of information to reason deductively.

Historical context

Not all essay questions will have a particularly relevant historical context. The essential issue to consider in this section of the essay formula is why the topic your addressing has become important in Psychology. With essay questions on intelligence or personality you will find a lot of material that describes how people approached these matters in the past. All you are doing is setting the scene and easing your reader into your more complex discussion, so be very brief.

Do not fall into the temptation of presenting your essay as the chronological events of the topic's development unless you are specifically asked to do so or because the development of the issue has some relevance to your argument. You will reach your word limit very quickly and not develop an argument.

3.3.6 Conclusions

You don't need to arrive at a firm conclusion—you rarely will in Psychology. In terms of the legal analogy, it is probably sufficient to create significant doubt in the mind of the jurors. You do this by convincing your audience that debate exists, that there is merit in a number of approaches to the subject matter, that one line of research seems to dominate, that previous lines of thought have significant hurdles to their development and so on. The point is to reason well to some end. The conclusion should follow naturally from the material you have considered and the argument you have developed. Thus, never introduce new material in your conclusion.

Avoid saying 'further research in this field is needed before the issue will be settled'. Instead, suggest reasons why it's important that further investigation take place and the issue settled. The grading you will receive for your conclusion is shown in the table below.

Conclusion	Grading
No conclusion	D
Concluding statement with new material	C
A statement of what you covered in the essay	B/A
A statement that develops from your argument and concisely summarises the findings of your research	A/A+

3.4 Essay style

An author's style comes from the emphasis of the writing techniques. Do not set out to create a style. You can adopt a particular style from another author. Unlike taking their ideas and representing them as your own, adopting their style is quite legitimate. Do not copy the style represented here as this Guide has been written. There are much better examples to follow that you will find when reading texts and journal articles. Do not copy your textbook's style. Textbook chapters are not essays!

There is one special warning about style. Formal writing is not necessarily pompous, despite being formal. Do not attempt to use sophisticated language to create a sophisticated style. A sophisticated style can use very simple language by exploiting sophisticated techniques of signposting, citing material and critically appraising theory (see pp. 85–86). The best ideas are expressed simply. The task is to convince your audience, not baffle them.

One good rule of thumb applies: 'be very boring!'. If you start out with flare and enthusiasm for style, you may get torn to shreds by the marker who can misinterpret the use of your style in your writing. For example, a journalist can misinterpret enthusiasm for a subject and put things in writing that with sober reflection would not have been said 'quite like that'. The boring article is better than the embarrassing one! So it is with the essay, although if you get the fundamentals right it will not be boring. It's best to limit any flare in your writing to opening statements, then you won't go too far wrong.

3.5 Things to avoid

■

> Do not put statements in the negative form. And don't start sentences with a conjunction. If you reread your work, you will find on rereading that a great deal of repetition can be avoided by rereading and editing. Never use a long word when a diminutive one will do. Unqualified superlatives are the worst of all. De-accession euphemisms. If any word is improper at the end of a sentence, a linking verb is. Avoid trendy locutions that sound flaky. Last, but not least, avoid clichés like the plague.
> *William Safire*

3.5.1 Personal pronouns

Avoid expressions such as 'I think that …' or 'My argument will detail four components of the theory …' or 'I will explain …'. There is no valid reason for dropping personal pronouns to index ownership of your ideas just because established authors do this all the time. However, it takes a sophisticated writing style to pull it off in a formal context so the problem is probably one of gaining some experience before attempting it. If you do try to use the personal pronoun, it may come across to the reader like the defence lawyer saying 'Well, I've examined the evidence and I think he's not guilty'. The difficulty is the defence lawyer is less than objective. Similarly, you will come across as less than objective if you personalise your argument. A better approach is to detach yourself from the statements. Here are some examples of how to do so:

- 'I think that ...' becomes 'It is reasonable to suppose that ...'
- 'My argument evaluates ...' becomes 'The argument evaluates ...'
- 'I will explain ...' becomes 'An explanation for ... is offered ...'
- My conclusion ...' becomes 'Therefore ...'

3.5.2 Researchers' titles

It's annoying to see a statement such as 'Researcher, Psychologist, Dr Peter James Johnson, PhD, of Northern Lights University, in the United States, recently found that ...'. There are variations on this that have less information, such as 'Dr Peter Johnson (1999) found ...' or 'Researcher, Johnson (1999) found ...'. Some people are tempted to write like this because journalists report research this way but this is wrong in formal writing.

The correct way to reference this would be 'Johnson (1999) found ...'. The reader does not need to know that Johnson is a researcher (the citation is to Johnson's research, thus he's a researcher). No one cares whether Johnson (1999) had a PhD or a medical degree; it does not help the argument. The issue is always the credibility of the research, not the credibility of the researcher. The same applies to the fact that the research was conducted at Northern Lights University in the United States. There might be an occasion when it is important to point out that the research was conducted in the United States. Then you might say 'In the United States, Johnson (1999) found ...'.

3.5.3 Emotive language

There is a language to arguments just as there is a language for Psychology and the presentation of research reports. This language is so old it still contains some Latin expressions that tend to confuse people when they first start out. A few common ones are listed in Table 3.2. The first rule of argumentation is to avoid emotive language. It's wrong to state that an argument is interesting (it may be to you), that facts are fascinating, clever, insightful, ingenious and so on. Worse still, it's wrong to write that an argument is stupid, ridiculous, foolish, inane or facile.

Even if you believe that an argument is appallingly bad, you must avoid the temptation of saying so—especially in tutorials when your colleagues state seemingly bad arguments. Most arguments can be defended on some interpretation that you haven't considered, so you need to state your point in a neutral way in case a point that you haven't considered comes back at you and then you look foolish. Thus, arguments can be flawed, invalid, misleading, limited, unclear and equivocal. An argument can be useful, valid and informative. Whenever you comment on an argument, make sure you give a reason why it's informative or useful; or if it's bad, why it's misleading, limited or flawed.

Table 3.2 Commonly used Latin expressions

Expression	Meaning	Example
Ceteris paribus	All other things being equal.	Given the opportunity, ceteris paribus, I can jump 3 metres.
A fortiori	With stronger force of argument.	I cannot jump 4 metres, a fortiori, I cannot jump 6 metres.
Ex hypothesi	As set out hypothetically.	According to prior research, people can typically jump 2–3 metres without difficulty. We required participants to jump 2 metres, which, ex hypothesi, they should have been able to achieve.
Inter alia	Among other things.	Jumping, swimming and running are, inter alia, some of the best things to do for fitness.
Ad infinitum	Continuing on and on forever. Often used to describe an infinite regress.	Without stopping for a break our participants would have enjoyed jumping so much they would have continued ad infinitum.
Ad hominem	Argument directed against the person (never use this).	Walton's jumping has jiggered his brain and he's a lousy jumper anyway.
A priori	What comes before (without the benefit of evidence or testing).	We have reason to assume a priori that people can jump at least 2 metres because of their muscular formation.
Sine qua non	Without which nothing.	Strong legs are the sine qua non for jumping lengthy distances.

3.5.4 Plagiarism

■

> If you steal from one author it's plagiarism; if you steal from many it's research.
> *Wilson Mizner*

Plagiarism has several forms but one simple idea underlies the concept. If you take an author's idea, argument, sentence, graph, table or particular expression and represent it as your own, then you have broken a simple rule. The rule is that you must acknowledge the source of the information that you have acquired in your case or your argument. This issue does not need to be examined here because the information above explains how to acknowledge your sources, and make sure you point, cite and quote appropriately. The work of others *is the evidence of your case* and should not be buried or absorbed within your argument. You get credit for representing, appraising, criticising and using the work of others to develop your case—that's the game. The one requirement is that you acknowledge that work appropriately.

Sometimes work is absorbed unintentionally. Avoid the lazy option of rephrasing what others have said. Instead, briefly describe what it is the authors say (and provide the reference) and then comment on the adequacy or usefulness of their contribution. If you are tempted to take the material for your own use, it must be because you like it for a particular reason. State the reason. It might be that the authors you are quoting or citing simply present the most succinct, clear, well-reasoned, sophisticated or learned account. Say this! Then write the about the significance of their contribution.

3.5.5 Sexism, racism and bigotry

You should avoid all forms of bigotry in your writing. It's simple really. Imagine your audience is a set of jurors from a wide range of social backgrounds and ethnicities and have mixed gender. You have to reach that audience and convince it of your case. You will struggle if you insult these people by being insensitive to their social or cultural background or their gender. It's not a matter of a perspective on political correctness or some fleeting stylistic requirement of writing s/he, she or he, or a mixed balance of both she and he. The requirement stems from the purpose of writing your essay. You are trying to hold your readers' attention and convince them of your argument.

- Never use 'he' as the third person singular pronoun. Wherever possible recast the sentence in the plural to use 'they' or 'their'.
- You may use 'she or he', 'he or she' or an equal balance of both 'he' and 'she' throughout.
- Using 'she or he' or 's/he' are not recommended. These are clumsy expressions that with a bit of practice can be avoided.
- The word 'mankind' should be replaced with 'people'.

3.5.6 Horrible formatting: headings

Never present a heading or subheading with a font or adjustment to the typeface as this is unnecessary and looks silly (see Fig. 3.2). One typeface only is sufficient. It is your argument and its supporting evidence that gets you your grade, not your formatting.

It looks really silly
AND IS UNNECESSARY
THIS IS NOT CORRECT BECAUSE IT USES THREE ADJUSTMENTS TO THE TYPEFACE

Fig. 3.2 Never use a mixture of typefaces in your headings

There are particular rules for how headings are formatted. Researchers in Psychology follow the conventions of the American Psychological Association (APA), who list out the rules in the APA Manual. Figures 3.3 and 3.4 show two examples: one for essays and one for research reports. There are several variations depending on the number of levels of heading you use. The rule you want to apply is to keep your headings very simple.

The First Main Heading goes in the Centre with Initial Upper Case for the Main Words and Proper Nouns

Your Name or Student Number

The First Main Heading goes in the Centre with Initial Upper Case for the Main Words and Proper Nouns

<u>A specific heading</u>

Text follows one the next line having an indent to start the paragraph.

Subheading. Text follows the subheading as if it were part of the paragraph.

Subheading. Text follows the subheading.

Conclusions

References

Fig. 3.3 Examples of heading for an essay

The First Main Heading goes in the Centre with Initial Upper Case for the Main Words and Proper Nouns

Your Name or Student Number

Abstract

The First Main Heading goes in the Centre with Initial Upper Case for the Main Words and Proper Nouns

Text starts here and continues

Method

Participants

   Student protestors in Australia

   Student protestors in New Zealand

Materials

Results

Discussion

Conclusions

References

Fig. 3.4 Example of headings for a research report

3.5.7 Bullet points, lists and the short paragraph

As mentioned above, the short paragraph does not belong to formal writing. This is important to remember because students often write variations on the short paragraph. Modern business language seems to demand short statements, often numbered, and stated very directly with simple language.

The two line paragraph is used for issuing an instruction and comes across as saying 'I can't be bothered explaining this, just do it'. Anyone who has ever received a job application rejection letter will understand this. The two line statement will have an impact on the marker similar to such a letter. In formal writing it is rare that anything will be asserted so bluntly, especially in Psychology. The requirement that you reference assertions ensures that each point you make has some evidential support or some argument that supports it.

If the statements you want to make seem necessary but are trivial or tangential to your discussion, then outline them very generally and point to a reference that does provide a detailed explanation. Then summarise briefly what that reference contains, how it expands out that material and the contribution that reference makes.

Never use bullet points, whether in a list that is numbered or with dots, dashes, diamonds or stars. They do not belong to formal writing. If you must write a numbered list, always do so within a paragraph. For example: (1) is your first point; (2) is your second point; (3) is your third point. The use of short paragraphs and bullet points will steer you towards a disastrous grade. Even if you understand the issues, research well and produce a really good argument, it must be presented appropriately.

3.6 Referencing

The references section at the end of your essay contains *all* the references you have referred to with your in-text referencing. Never include a reference that is not an in-text reference.

The list is presented alphabetically according to the surname of the author. There are numerous rules, such as for placing initials, commas, underlying titles or journals. Bond and McConkey (2000) has examples of the types of reference you will encounter in its references section. The easiest way for you to get it right is to use this reference section as a set of examples of the general rules.

The following gives an account of the main ones you will need. Included is an account of how to reference pages from the World Wide Web.

3.6.1 Books

General formula
Surname, Initials. (Year). <u>Title of book.</u> City of publication: Publisher.

Examples
Haefele, J. W. (1962). <u>Creativity and innovation</u>. New York: Reinbold.
Moghaddam, F. M., Taylor, D. M., & Wright, S. C. (1993). <u>Social psychology in cross cultural perspective.</u> New York: Freeman.
Plomin, R., De Fries, J. C., & McClearn, G. E. (1990). <u>Behavioural genetics: A primer</u> (2nd ed.). New York: Freeman.

3.6.2 Edited books

General formula
Surname, Initials. (Year). Title of the chapter. In Initials. Surname of Editor (Ed.), <u>Title of the edited book</u> (pp. 00–00). City of publication: Publisher.

Examples
Petty, R. E., & Cacioppo, J. T. (1981). The elaboration likelihood model of persuasion. In L. Berkowitz (Ed.), <u>Advances in experimental social psychology</u> (Vol. 19). Orlando, FL: Academic Press.

3.6.3 Dictionaries and encyclopaedias

Stein, J. (Ed.). (1982). <u>The Random House dictionary of the English language</u> (unabridged ed.). New York: Random House.

3.6.4 Journal articles

General formula
Surname, Initials. (Year). Title of the article: Perhaps it has a subheading. <u>Journal the Article Appears In, volume</u> (number), pages.

Examples
Hardaway, R. A. (1991). Subliminally activated symbiotic fantasies: Facts and artefacts. <u>Psychological Bulletin, 107,</u> 177–95.
McKenna, F. P., Stanier, R. A., & Lewis, C. (1991). Factors underlying self-assessment of driving skills in males and females. <u>Accident Analysis and Prevention, 23</u> (4), 45–52.

Note: When you do not put the volume number in the reference you put 'pp.' before the page numbers. When a volume number appears you omit the 'pp.' and just write the page numbers.

3.6.5 Web page material

In August 1999, the APA issued new guidelines for citing electronic resources. You can look up the technical details of other materials at: http://www.apa.org/journals/webref.html
   To reference an entire website, it's sufficient to give the address of the site in the text in the same way as the APA's guidelines. The APA Manual cites the example below as a way of listing a page from which you draw information. This is how it would appear in your references:

Jacobson, J. W., Mulick, J. A., & Schwartz, A. A. (1995). A history of facilitated communication: Science, pseudoscience, and antiscience: Science working group on facilitated communication. <u>American Psychologist, 50,</u> 750–65. Retrieved January 25, 1996 from the World Wide Web: http://www.apa.org/journals/jacobson.html

General formula
Surname, Initials. (Year). <u>Title of work.</u> Page {if possible}. Retrieved date from the World Wide Web: specify path.

The imprint: where to find the components of the reference for a book

Books, edited volumes, dictionaries and encyclopaedias

Take any book. If you turn over the title page you will find what is called the imprint. It's even in this book. The imprint is the publisher's details along with statements of copyright, printer's details, the ISBN number and information about the publication of the book. You need to find two things on this page: the date of publication and the publisher. The difficulty is that the other information has a potential to confuse you. The publisher will generally appear on the spine of the book and on the title page. It will appear again on the imprint, along with an obvious date of publication, generally somewhere around the copyright statement.

Turn to the title page for the author, title and the place of publication. Often places of publication appear as: 'London, Sydney, New York, Toronto'. Use the first place of publication listed. Now you have all the information. If you follow this through for this Guide you will find the reference details as:

Walton, D. (2000). <u>Studying psychological science: A guide to accompany Bond and McConkey, Psychological science: An introduction.</u> Sydney: McGraw-Hill.

Do not confuse the printer's details and place of printing with the publisher's details. It's easy to avoid because the words 'Printed in ...' always precede the printer's details.

Journals

Nowadays, journals generally place an almost complete reference to the article at the top left or top right of the first page of the article. This is done because people often interloan (photocopied and sent from another university or library) or photocopy articles for research purposes. This helps to keep track of the reference if the journal details accompany each article. If the information isn't on the first page of the article, then you will need to know the journal title, volume number, issue number and page numbers of the article. These are found on the front of the journal when it has not been bound. If you have a bound volume, go back in the volume until you find the cover of the issue your article appears in and the information will be obvious on the front of the journal.

3.7 Essentials of the referencing formulae

Figure 3.5 is a set of references with those things that people often overlook indicated. Take note of the components that are highlighted. The periods and commas are important; as is the order you put the information in. Note that the titles of articles and books reserve the upper case letter for only the first word and for proper nouns.

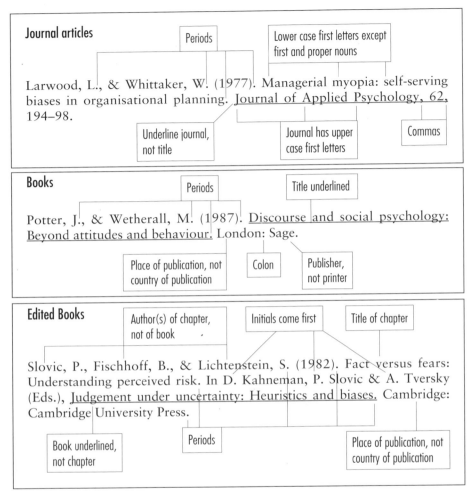

Fig. 3.5 How to reference journal articles, books and edited books

3.8 Frequently asked questions

Referencing is so complicated, how do I remember all the rules?

Don't bother. Your textbook has every type of reference listed in its reference section. Look up the references section, find an example of the type of reference you need to include and copy the formula it is applying. The same advice applies to in-text referencing.

Alternatively, how did you find the material or study you are referencing? With a reference? The references you acquire within Bond and McConkey (2000) will be accurately listed in the references section. Copy these references.

It's astonishing how often students fail to get the reference for their textbook correct and yet it's written down in their course materials, handouts and so on. Here it is again:

Bond, N., & McConkey, K. (Eds.). (2000). <u>Psychological science: An introduction</u>. Sydney: McGraw-Hill.

All the texts listed as recommended reading for the essay have gone from the library

True, they will disappear within a few hours of the list being presented to a class. Sometimes lecturers will hold some back for reserved loan. Read pages 98–100.

I'm hopeless at grammar. Help!

Look at the back of a good dictionary for a guide to the basics of grammar. Get help by reading specialised books that describe the basic rules of grammar and proper sentence construction. Get someone else to proofread your work. Keep it simple!

Can I go over the word limit?

Follow the rules you are given. Generally you can exceed the word limit by no more than 5–10% of the limit. If it's 1000 words, do not write any more than 1050–1100 words. Start sacrificing material by asking yourself whether you really need it to make your case. Consider pointing as an option for summarising your research citations.

Can I go under the word limit?

Perhaps, but a similar rule to that above applies. Don't go under by more than 5–10%. If you need to pad out the essay, do so with more citations and more evidence. Comment on something that could do with more explanation. Do not pad out an essay by extending your opening paragraph or conclusions; these should be brief.

I cannot proofread and my spell checker doesn't get all the errors

A computer spell checker and grammar checker will never be able to remove all errors. Get someone else to read your work. Read the work aloud to check for fluency of language use. This may sound silly but experienced writers do it, and once it doesn't sound silly it probably won't be silly to read.

I don't have a computer, word processor or typewriter, and I can't type anyway. Can I write it out by hand?

It depends on the marker, probably, but you will need to check. Make sure it's neat handwriting. Remember, it takes twice as long to read and mark a handwritten essay compared with a typewritten one.

What's 'et al.' stand for?

'Et al.' means 'and others'. The reference may first appear as McCormick, Walkey & Green (1986) and later as McCormick et al. (1986). The use of et al. is to avoid the clumsy repetition of long lists of researchers. When you have more than two researchers in the study you cite, list them all out for the first time you refer to that study, and thereafter just the first author followed by et al.

What about a bibliography?

A bibliography is a list of informative sources and materials, it is not a set of references, despite being composed of them. Markers get upset when you put 'Bibliography' because you are inviting them to read material relevant to the topic. Other subjects may insist on bibliographies; in Psychology these are called 'references'.

What about footnotes?

You may use footnotes but use them very sparingly. Never use them to replace in-text referencing. Other subjects do this but this is wrong in Psychology. Generally, a footnote is used to clarify an issue that is not central to your main point.

What does 'sic' mean?

The use of 'sic' indicates to a reader that an error of grammar or content in the original source that is quoted is not due to an error in the present production of the material. Put simply, it means 'I know there's an error, but it's not mine!'.

In an in-text reference, where does the date go?

If you are going to describe the study in some detail, put 'Svenson (1981) found …'. If you are pointing to the study or putting it in a list it will probably appear as (Svenson, 1981).

What about bullet points?

Never present material within your essay in bullet points or numbering in lists. If you must list out a series of points, then they should appear as: (1) first point ...; (2) second point ...; (3) third point, etc. These points should be listed within a paragraph that introduces them and then explains their significance.

I can copy my friend's essay from last year and pass with an A! Why bother with this?

There is a difference between taking shortcuts and cheating. Writing is a skill that must be learnt over time. Sometimes you have to risk a poor grade to adapt a style, break a bad writing habit, explore a new style and develop critical thinking beyond that which is measured by the ordinary standards of essay marking guides. You cannot learn these things vicariously (you won't learn about vicarious learning either, unless you read your text).

Firstly, secondly, thirdly ...

There is no way to firstly do something. You do something first. Replace 'firstly' with 'first'. For example, in your outline it appears: 'First, the arguments for the dopamine hypothesis are considered ... Second, research supporting the arguments is examined ... Third, the applications are proposed ... Finally, the conclusion reached is ...'.

Do I change American spelling in the things I quote?

No. Leave a quotation exactly as it is written. If you need to avoid some ambiguity of confusion in the quotation that results from an Americanism or other cultural difference, use square brackets. For example, you might write: Smith (1999, p.12) states 'The rate of accidents in 50 mph [80 kph] zones is reducing due to the new initiatives of the California Highway Patrol'.

How can I avoid absorbing and presenting the information of others I read? At what point do the ideas I read become mine and legitimately written as my own in the essay?

The words and expressions of others are theirs if they are an original idea of theirs or a unique expression that is clearly theirs. It is conceivable that you might accidentally repeat the same sentence of some writer. Nonetheless, the odds are astronomically large that you will find the same beginning sentence in any two different books you pick up in the library. As stated above, you will get credit for presenting the material that is the work of experts in the field you are writing about, provided you reference that work. That's how you avoid the problem. You get credit for organising the material. What is yours alone is the organisation of the material—that's the novel contribution you make.

3.9 Eleven easy steps for researching and writing essays

Step 1 Read the question

Write down terms that seem related to those central concepts in the question.

- Look up the glossary of Bond and McConkey (2000) and examine the key terms of your question. Read these glossary terms, briefly scan the subject index for those terms and read those pages you are referred to.
- Look up the author index. Match the corresponding names in your question to those pages references in Bond and McConkey.
- Examine the verbs and connectives in the question.

Favourite forms of questions

- <u>Describe</u> A <u>and</u> give examples.
- <u>Contrast</u> A with B <u>and</u> give examples.
- <u>Critically appraise</u> the evidence for A theory.
- <u>Is</u> A sufficient for B?

Is the question one of evidence, definitions or theory? Must you give examples of a lot of research? Is the essay an argument with research used to illustrate the argument? Is the essay one about presenting research to develop an argument?

Step 2 Encyclopaedias of Psychology

Encyclopaedias are useful for providing a general overview of your topic and will generally contain an almost essay-like answer to many questions you are asked to answer. They often point out a few key theories and studies that will help you too. Read one of these for a general introduction to your question.

However, some questions are a bit curly for this step to operate effectively. For example, a favourite question is 'Is Psychology a science?'.

Step 3 Seek a general text

Try typing in the key terms into your library's computerised catalogue. Are the books already gone? Browsing the shelves in that area is the next step. If you cannot find a good dedicated text, go for general texts. General texts are much better and more informative at an introductory level than those books your computer catalogue will provide. If the essay is in an area of Social Psychology, find a Social Psychology text. If the essay is about some aspect of brain function, find a Biological Psychology text. That text will probably be designed for stage two or three students and will have a much more developed discussion than you need to answer the question. Still, it will be far less developed than those you will get from a text dedicated to the specific subject you are asked to write about (and therefore a lot less reading too!). Read the text for its summaries of research or evaluation of theories.

Remember to spend some time examining the introduction of that text for the definitions and the discussion of fundamental concepts.

Step 4 Examine your reading list and text for the fundamentals

Take notes of the fundamentals! Gather the material from the reading list. If you don't get a reading list, examine your textbook and a specialised text for the main theories and studies they discuss. You should attempt to find one or two of the main research-based papers and any review articles referred to in the discussions your text outlines. These sources are the key to the information essential to answering the question in the best possible way. Don't try to read everything. Your reference list will be quite lengthy if you get material from one or two key works: your text, a specialised text, an encyclopaedia and a dictionary of Psychology.

Taking notes

What is the essence of the theoretical controversy? (Often this *is* the question you are asked to write about.)

- What research has been done?
- Why was the research done?
- Was the research exploratory, experimental, quasi-experimental?
- How recently was the research done?
- What conclusions were drawn?

The trick here is to gather one or two pieces of information from each source that is listed on a reading list. In this way, your examiner will recognise that you have read widely. You will be surprised, though, that after labouring through articles and books, taking notes and expending an enormous amount of effort in the final draft, that effort is represented by a few lines in the essay. The point is that width is better than depth at this level. When you only have to write 1000 or so words, gaining a broad overview is much better than going into detail. Thus, it's better to have a broad range of things to reference and point to than one article you discuss at length because you spent 4 hours reading it.

Step 5 Plan your argument

Develop a working plan about what conclusion you might reach. Write that conclusion down. We sometimes hold conclusions vaguely and when we try to express the idea we find we cannot do so. See Chapter 5 for some clues on good arguments and how to appraise theoretical statements.

Step 6 Collect sufficient evidence

Re-examine the evidence. Can you make your case? Will the evidence support your conclusion? Consider how strong your conclusion is. Can you hem it in a bit without making it seem too lame? If you need more information, re-examine the textbook. Note that the text does not necessarily present all the connections between subject matter conveniently. Do not bias your case by ignoring evidence that goes against it (see pp. 95–96). If you cannot make the argument you first decided on, consider limiting your conclusions.

Step 7 Find the extra pieces for the A grade

Read beyond your reading list and your text. Get one or two new pieces of information from any of the following:

1. Local data. If in your previous reading you noted a general fact drawn from American or British literature, then try to determine the local Australian statistics or facts. For example, an essay that deals with prejudice will draw on evidence gathered about racism in America and Britain. The simple facts about the percentage of minorities making up Australian society are an almost essential detail you should include in your essay. Yearbooks generally have summaries of a lot of interesting facts and figures relevant to Psychology and problems that Psychology addresses. These facts and figures make for good opening statements.
2. A specialised text's summary of relevant research.
3. The introduction of a journal article that seems from your previous research to be cited often and central to the question. These articles often summarise previous research very well.
4. Applications of the research drawn from Psychology. Research and theory almost always attempt to change everyday practice. Can you find any information about the question's application? For example, if the essay question is about intelligence, try to find information about intelligence quotient (IQ) testing in schools, employment selection and so on. Often applications in some countries seem to have no real application in others. For example, the polygraph is used in America but not often in Australia, Britain and New Zealand.

Step 8 The writing phase

Sketch out a draft plan like that described as the essay formula. If the essay is 18 paragraphs, make sure you say all you want to say in 18 paragraphs. If you collected 20 studies on an issue, you will need to summarise them generally and invoke the in-text referencing techniques of pointing, citing research and listing research as evidence.

Step 9 First draft, second draft, third draft ...

Follow the ordering of paragraph writing listed in the essay formula. Students hate writing drafts, which is why the essay formula is a draft of sorts. Write up your first draft according to the formula but remember it's a guide. Your question may be very different and you will need to adjust it according to the flow of your argument. A sculptor must work with the material and allow it sometimes to dominate the course of things for a time before the sculptor takes control again. It's the same when writing essays. Essay writing is an art.

Step 10 Final draft: revise for clarity, completeness of argument, typographical errors and word length

In practice, most authors will write anywhere between four and 30 drafts of an essay before it is accepted for publication. In reality, students do not have the time to polish an essay. However, you must get someone else to read it first. Or, you can endure the reflexive embarrassment of standing alone in your room and reading the essay aloud to your mirror, pet, poster or whatever. It does work. Always plan to write two or three drafts of your essay.

Step 11 Tick 'yes' to all the questions in the essay checklist

3.10 The essay checklist

Some of the items on the essay checklist require your judgment whereas others are simply statements about whether or not you have done the things you really need to do. The questions do not appear in any particular order of importance so that you move through and answer all of them. If you answer 'yes' to all the questions, then you will fly in with an A+. You will not fail an essay if you can answer 'yes' to all the questions. Once you have answered 'yes' to all the questions, hand your essay in. Good luck!

Essay checklist

	Yes	No
1. The question was examined to identify the components for discussion.	❏	❏
2. The question is answered using evidence and theory drawn from Psychology.	❏	❏
3. There is not too much material from another discipline such as sociology, philosophy or biology.	❏	❏
4. A conclusion that relates to the question is developed.	❏	❏
5. The conclusion is concise but not definitive.	❏	❏
6. Quotations are not overused.	❏	❏
7. The essay's argument is briefly outlined in the 'signposting paragraph'.	❏	❏
8. The key terms were defined in a paragraph that evaluated the limitations of several definitions.	❏	❏
9. Varieties of referencing techniques are developed, such as listing, pointing and citing.	❏	❏
10. All quotations are evaluated and critically appraised.	❏	❏
11. The conclusion recognises the limitations of the argument developed in the essay.	❏	❏
12. All references are listed in the references section.	❏	❏
13. Only the references actually referred to in the essay are in the references section.	❏	❏
14. The essay has a wide margin for the marker's comments.	❏	❏
15. The essay accomplishes all that is stated in the signposting section.	❏	❏
16. I have read the essay aloud or given it to someone else to check for fluency, grammar and spelling.	❏	❏
17. The headings are in a simple format and do not alter the typeface more than once.	❏	❏
18. There are no bullet points or lists of points in the essay.	❏	❏
19. The essay has page numbers, and a student number or name.	❏	❏
20. Each paragraph attempts to address a single issue or theme.	❏	❏
21. The short sentence never appears in the essay at any point.	❏	❏
22. The writing is formal but not pompous or unnecessarily complex.	❏	❏
23. The references are all in APA style.	❏	❏
24. I know the rules for the use of the possessive apostrophe and I have applied them throughout or avoided its use altogether.	❏	❏
25. The references section is not labelled 'bibliography'.	❏	❏
26. There are no contractions, such as 'wouldn't' or 'can't'.	❏	❏
27. A variety of evidence is introduced to support the argument.	❏	❏
28. The essay is evenly balanced in its critique of the evidence.	❏	❏
29. The essay is no more than +/− 10% of the word limit.	❏	❏
30. There is evidence that I read beyond the material in the reading list to find evidence for the argument.	❏	❏
31. The practical applications of this knowledge, evidence or argument are discussed in the essay.	❏	❏
32. I have not used sexist language or represented the work of others as my own.	❏	❏

Isn't this a lot of effort? I have other essays to write and it's only worth 10%

This is true in part. Remember when you first learned to drive and you had to keep telling yourself 'change down to second when going around a corner'? For those who don't remember that, can you remember how you had to keep telling yourself about the steps for logging on to your computer (perhaps you even wrote them down)? The best approach to complex tasks is to break them down into steps and consider each step, one at a time. You will do this naturally in time, just as you drive a car without thinking too much about each step in the process. Writing is a complex task! Some people don't believe this because they have spent 15 years writing things before they reach university. You may get away with adequate grades in your first year without all this effort, but your grades may decline over time. In your second and third year the things outlined here are not just desirable, they are expected.

CHAPTER 4

RESEARCH REPORT WRITING

OVERVIEW

4.1 The research report formula
4.2 Refinements to the formula for research report writing
4.3 The introduction
4.4 The hypothesis
4.5 Methods: sample, materials and procedures
4.6 Data presentation
4.7 The discussion
4.8 The abstract
4.9 Things to avoid
4.10 The research report checklist
4.11 Frequently asked questions

INTRODUCTION

As with essay writing, there is a formula for writing laboratory reports. However, the essay writing formula is a guide only and has a loose structure that may need to be adjusted depending on the question asked and the requirements of your examiner. With research report writing, the formula is very clear. Research report writing follows the structure of a scientific journal article, which psychologists write often and philosophers probably rarely write. Research report writing is the skill in which psychologists are the experts.

You will write a report because you have conducted some practical exercise, either because you were instructed to collect some data or you conducted an experiment in a tutorial or laboratory setting. Generally, this will involve the replication of some other study or relate clearly to an issue that will lead to reasonably predictable results. However, be aware that most research report writing does not start with the collection of data. Almost all research starts from research conducted in the library, by reading the literature within an area and developing a research idea, which is then formed into an hypothesis or set of hypotheses. Only then is the idea tested and ultimately written up into a research report.

It may be apparent now why in Introductory Psychology, researching and writing essays develops fundamental skills. Without those fundamental skills you would probably never reach the point of researching ideas or being able to represent them in a research report.

Many of the components of research writing have already been introduced. In particular, from the essay writing formula you already know about opening statements, scene setting, signposting, referencing and conclusions, along with some general rules of what to avoid in formal writing. All of these points apply here. However, some additional components need to be introduced that are particular to report writing: the abstract, hypotheses, methods, results, and the presentation of data.

4.1 The research report formula

As was the case with essay writing, let us assume your report is to be 2000 words and you have 20–30 paragraphs. Even with a larger word limit, you can have more paragraphs here than you would apportion to an essay because the structure dictates that you must include some material, sometimes in short paragraphs, and so often you will write quite concise statements that have a clear meaning without much introduction. For example, writing your hypothesis is a paragraph but it should be contained in less than 50 words. For this reason, an approximate word limit on each section is outlined in Figure 4.1, given a report length of 2000 words.

■

Brevity is the soul of wit.   *William Shakespeare*

Special consideration should be given to those reports that are written up during a 2–4 hour laboratory exercise. Some laboratory experiments might require a very brief report, perhaps not exceeding 500–1000 words. In that case, you will have guidance from an instructor as to what is expected. The same rules apply, although you will sacrifice much of the introductory material and focus on the presentation of the exercise in the results and discussion sections.

When word limits are imposed, remember the techniques of pointing and listing discussed in Chapter 3. Much of the introductory section is made up of a description of past research. If you developed a short paragraph that lists or points to other research after your scene-setting paragraph, then you will reduce the outline's word length to 1200 words easily.

	Cover page	Title		
		Student details		
	Abstract*	A summary of the report's aim, main findings, argument and conclusions.	27	100–150
	Introduction*			
1	Scene setting	Broad statement about the topic of investigation	26	100
2–6	Other research	A description and evaluation of other research	1–5	500
7	This research	Aim of this research. What is the problem that this research aims to solve?	7	
8		Contribution of this research. Why is this research different from past research?	8	100
9		Limitations of this research. What is the research not designed to accomplish? Often this includes being representative of everyone because the experiment does not operate on a random sample.	9	
10	Hypothesis*	A concise, exact statement of what is being tested and what the expected result will be.	6	50
	Method			
11	Sample/ participants*	Who took part in the experiment? Age, sex, occupation, how they were selected, whom do they represent. If the research involved animals, then state the animal, weight, sex, condition (starved of food for 24 hours, prevented from exercise, etc.).	10	100
12–13	Apparatus/ materials*	You need to describe the materials you used whether physical (Skinner box, tachistoscopes, etc.) or not (survey questions, interview questions, etc.).	11	100
14	Procedure/ manipulation*	Describe the independent and dependent variables.	12	100
	Results			
15	Data tables, figures and graphs*	Contingency tables, bar graphs, line graphs scatter graphs, etc. Choose an appropriate way to represent your data. Only include what is necessary, never include your raw data.	13	50
16	Statistics*	Describe what sort of analysis and represent the results of that analysis. Always write a description in words following your presentation of statistical results.	14	100

Fig. 4.1 The research writing formula

◀

		Discussion*		
17	Restate the hypothesis	Briefly describe the hypothesis, do not duplicate the same presentation as before. You might loosen the hypothesis out to an aim if appropriate.	16	50
18–20	Restate the main results	What were the main findings?	17	150
21–24	Explain the results	What reasons can be given for the pattern of results? Do the results lead to any reasonable conclusion?	18–24	200
25	Qualifications and limitations*	What things might have interfered with the results? How could you improve the study (e.g. sample size, selection of subjects, distractions in the research environment, cultural, social, gender or age effects)?	25	100
26	Theoretical significance	Does this research support a theory or go against one? Is there an adequate theory for these results to fit with (links to your introduction)?	26	200
27	Conclusions	Briefly conclude by summarising the significance of the research and results.	27	100
		References	28	
	Appendices	Data tables, surveys, question items, schedules, mathematics or anything too lengthy to include in the report, including notes if they are reasonable.	29	

*Only those sections with asterisks are discussed in the text. The other components have already been outlined in Chapter 3. This is particularly true of referencing and in-text referencing. Those who have not read Chapter 3 should consult it before attempting to write a research-based assignment.

Fig. 4.1 The research writing formula *(continued)*

4.2 Refinements to the formula for research report writing

When discussing essay writing, we regarded the refinements as ways of improving a basic formula in order to improve a grade by making a better essay. The essay formula was regarded as a poor alternative to the refinements. Here, however, do not mistake the formula for a set of minimum requirements that can be abandoned as your skill improves. The research report formula is set down fairly rigidly. It would take an advanced understanding of Psychology and scientific report writing before attempting any deviation from the main outline. In particular, you must set out the headings in bold. Every research report will present sections labelled: Introduction, Method, Results, Discussion and References.

4.3 The introduction[11]

Your introduction is meant to develop an argument for the reason you investigated the issue with data collection and analysis. In terms of the detective analogy used in Chapter 3, it is the presentation of your 'hunch' about who committed the crime. Here, however, you are not trying to convince the judge and jury, rather someone like the police chief. The argument you are putting forward is one like 'I need more resources to gather the crucial evidence'. Better still, 'the case can be solved beyond doubt with a piece of new evidence'. Of course, by doing the research and gathering the evidence, it is hoped that you are going to acquire that evidence.

An introduction is a mini essay, except that it does not lead to a conclusion; it leads to a question or an hypothesis. You still need to define your terms, signpost and start with a catchy opening paragraph. Some people use the expression 'literature review' to describe the introduction. These people recognise that the main idea is to identify why the question addressed in the research has not been answered to this date. Thus, it's a review of research. You must explain the approaches already adopted addressing the issue, explain why they don't satisfactorily provide an answer to your research question and describe why your approach is unique. For example, it might be that no one has ever attempted to ask the question with an Australian sample. A sample of Australian students may provide data that are quite different to those developed in America, where the previous research might have been performed. Such would be the case, perhaps, with questions concerning attitudes, leisure activities, values and expectations.

Writing your introduction to review the literature requires the techniques of in-text referencing (citing, pointing, listing, quoting) that were explained in Chapter 3. Remember that you are building up to a question or an hypothesis. The crucial question to ask of your introduction is 'Does it explain why I decided to conduct the research?'. Note that you will have to pretend that your reason for doing the research is not because you have been directed to and that the assessment contributes to your overall grade (see table below).

Introduction	Grading
Introduction explains the aim of the research	D
Introduction defines key terms and the aim of the research	C/B
Introduction examines past research, theory, definitions and identifies a reason for the investigation	A/A+

---

[11] Although the abstract appears first in the report writing formula and in the final production of your report, it should be written last. See pp. 72–73 for help on writing an abstract.

4.4 The hypothesis

An hypothesis[12] or a set of hypotheses (plural) is the methodological formulation of an idea. It's the idea that you have that you want to test; it plays the leading part in the development, planning and writing of a research report. How ideas are developed is still a mystery to both psychologists and philosophers. Popper (1972), a philosopher who was interested in the function of hypotheses, wrote that: 'The initial stage, the act of conceiving or inventing a theory, seems to me neither to call for logical analysis nor is susceptible to it' (p. 31). Popper thought that psychologists would be best to investigate the notion. Essentially, there are no rules we know for conceiving an idea. On the other hand, once developed, how we present our idea and test it is a matter for which rules can be formulated. The scientific method, called the hypothetico-deductive method, outlines such rules and the notion of an hypothesis is central to this description of science.[13] It is this method, or a set of rules, which is outlined here.

■

When ideas fail, words come in very handy.   *Goethe*

Hypotheses are defined as 'Specified expectations about empirical reality, derived from propositions' (Babbie, 1995, p. 49). In fact, there are two types of hypothesis statements—a *research hypothesis* and a special hypothesis called the *null hypothesis*—but what we are concerned with for now is the research hypothesis. Let's unpack Babbie's statement, using the Oxford English dictionary for help:

Proposition: A statement or assertion.
Specified: Named or mentioned expressly.
Expectations: Regard as likely to occur in the future, particularly relating to an event or state of affairs.
Empirical: Based on acting on observation or experimentation, not on theory.

An hypothesis is a proposition that states exactly (specifically) what outcome of observation or testing is likely to occur from the process of experimenting or

---

[12] The 'an' in 'an hypothesis' seems strange to some people at first but is grammatically correct. You can also write, and say, 'a hypothesis'. You cannot say my 'hypothesises'; 'its hypotheses'. You should be careful with the use of: datum/data; stratum/strata; criterion/criteria; thesis/theses; schema/schemata.

[13] This theory is not the only description of the scientific process, nor is it without controversy. Still, for our purpose of designing and writing reports, its dominance necessitates the rules specified in this section.

observing a set of events. It is not an aim or desired outcome; for example, we may hold a desire to win the lottery without an expectation that we will win. When you write out your hypothesis it must be in the form of a tightly packed statement relating to the conditions of your experiment and a predicted result. Thus, the research aim:

'that gender is unrelated to anti-abortion attitudes'

is *not* an hypothesis. Whereas the following is an hypothesis:

'That males in a random sample of 50 subjects drawn from the university first-year enrolments will demonstrate a significant difference to females on a 12 point scale measuring attitudes towards abortions'

Features of a good hypothesis are:

- testability: that the measures specified are indeed tested in the experiment, and can be tested
- completeness: you should mention the conditions of the observation or experiment (e.g. 50 subjects whose attitudes towards abortion are measured on a 12 point scale). In most cases, you can describe a manipulation or an independent variable (e.g. gender) and the expected outcome or effect on the dependent variable (attitude towards abortion).

Hypothesis presentation	Grading
No hypothesis stated	D
Hypothesis incomplete and more like a research aim	C/D
Hypothesis states expected results	B/A
Hypothesis states conditions of research and expected results as a concise proposition	A/A+

4.5 Methods: sample, materials and procedures

4.5.1 Sample/participants

Your sample may be a group of animals or a group of people (when talking about people they are participants). Generally, a sample is selected because it is thought to be representative of a broader population (e.g. of students, lawyers, the public, criminals, 18 year olds, etc.). A random sample means that everyone in the population of interest had an equal chance for inclusion in the sample. You will probably not obtain a random sample in your introductory year research assignments. If you do obtain a random sample, you need to state such here and your method of obtaining that sample: how you ensured everyone had equal opportunity for being included in the study.

Of more importance is the requirement to state the characteristics of your sample that might have an impact on the results you obtain. Age and gender often have the potential to impact on research findings, so these data are routinely collected and reported in this section. What you declare depends on the nature of your experiment or research. If the experiment deals with perception, say peripheral vision, then it's not important what sort of educational background the participants have but it's very important to note how many members of your sample wear corrective lenses. If the study is about attitudes towards drinking and driving, then it's very important to declare how many members do not drink but do drive, and how many drink but do not drive. Any feature of your sample that might impact on your predicted outcome should be declared.

4.5.2 Materials

A common mistake, even by experienced researchers, is to report that a survey sheet was handed out for participants to fill in. It's obvious that you are using a questionnaire because you will declare such in your introduction. It's even more obvious that participants filled it in; otherwise you would not be reporting the result of the research. However, some aspects of the questionnaire or survey must be presented. It's very important to describe the general form of the questions in the survey, what they intend to measure and how they were derived. You will generally be repeating the research of others. If so, you will need to indicate that the questionnaire was developed and used by someone else. Of course, you need to reference this source.

Other materials need explanation too. If you are using a piece of physical apparatus, such as a T-maze or a Skinner box, you will need to state this, but more importantly, you will need to describe the reinforcement used (water, condensed milk, etc.), the conditions of the animal (starved for 24 hours) and the reinforcement schedule.

4.5.3 Procedure/manipulation

It's very important to grapple with the concepts of dependent and independent variables. These are explained in Bond and McConkey (2000, p. P1.28). Most research depends on some sort of manipulation of a variable (the independent variable) but it's not always obvious what that might be. Surveys and questionnaires don't seem to rely on manipulation, whereas altering the length of time a subject looks at a figure on the computer screen is fairly obviously an experimental manipulation of some sort. The difficulty, then, is whether the length of time is a dependent or independent measure. Surveys do have manipulations but they occur in the analysis phase when, for example, males are compared to females for their response on other items.

Because the manipulation is often obscured in the research design, this section of the report declares the sorts of manipulations undertaken and often the independent and dependent variables are stated explicitly. The best way to outline the logic of your experiment is to define the independent variable first and then say what measures were used.

Thus, the procedure section isn't about what you did exactly—it's not about saying 'we handed out a 12 item survey' or 'we put the rat in the Skinner box'. It's about the design of your research—'that 12 items of the survey measured attitudes toward abortion' or 'reinforced bar pressing in a Skinner box on a fixed ratio schedule'. The procedure relates to your hypothesis and explains how it is that you set up your research to test your hunch about what people, or animals, will do given the conditions you put them in.

4.6 Data presentation

Data (datum in the singular) are the results of your study or investigation. These need to be represented to the reader of your report in some summary format. Different types of data require different ways of presentation. You can read about the different types of data in Chapter 2 of Bond and McConkey (2000). The biggest mistake made by introductory students is to present data in tables and graphs without offering a written explanation of the table or graph's contents. After you have presented your data in a graph or a table, you *must* write a small description of what the graph or table represents. These summaries offer the reader the most important information. When writing out these descriptions, imagine that readers do not have the graph in their copy of your report and that you are providing them with a brief outline of what it represents.

4.6.1 Tables

The best way to explain tables is by example. Figures 4.2 and 4.3 illustrate examples of tables. Some general rules about tables that you should adhere to are also provided. The data presented in Figure 4.2 are fictitious.

Table The frequency of speeding offences by gender and licence status for 9086 18–20 year old university students

Traffic offences	Males		Females	
	Licensed	Unlicensed	Licensed	Unlicensed
None	4567	689	2789	245
Speeding offences	457	190	78	71
Total	5024	879	2867	316

Fig. 4.2 An example of a contingency table

Points to note

1. Keep the table as simple as possible. Do not enclose it in a box and do not have lines running vertically through your table unless they are required to prevent some ambiguity.
2. Tables offer data. Figures offer some graphical illustration or model of some concept. Tables are called tables and numbered consecutively.
3. Your caption should offer a good description of your table's contents.

Often tables present the summary statistics of data collected. These might include the mean, medians and standard deviations. When some sort of estimation of the significance of a summary statistic is performed, a value on that estimate's associated distribution is given and a probability value is provided. If you conduct a series of *t*-tests (see pp. 127–31), for example, you might produce table such as that shown in Figure 4.3 taken from De Joy (1989).

Table Global perceptions of driving competency and accident risk

Measure	Mean rating	*t*	Percent optimistic
Driving safety	2.03 (2.34)	8.94*	75.5
Driving skill	3.01 (1.77)	17.56*	88.7
Accident likelihood	−1.38 (2.18)	−6.49*	54.3

*Standard deviations are presented in brackets. $p < 0.001$.

Fig. 4.3 An example of a data summary table

Points to note

1. Under your table you may provide asterisks or footnote markers to aid the reader in interpreting the meaning of your data summary.
2. Again, this table is very simple. The less complicated the table, the easier it will be to interpret.

4.6.2 Graphs

You will be introduced to a variety of graphs in your laboratory course. Graphs all do the same thing: they represent data and relationships between data. Graphs provide a description; they supplement a written description or a statistical analysis. Graphs are *not* your results; a graph will describe your results.

The following are rules for the presentation of graphs:

1. The independent variable is on the *x*-axis. The dependent variable is on the *y*-axis.
2. Legends appear within the dimensions of the graph (legends are sometimes called 'keys').

3. Bars should be easy to differentiate by their shading. (Black and white is fine, don't use patterns, and never use colour.)
4. A caption should be included that explains the graph and the sample size (e.g. $N = 238$).
5. Lines are smooth and sharp (i.e. not dotted).
6. Make sure your graph is large enough to be read easily.
7. Only use a graph if it is helpful; consider leaving it out if you describe the information in the text.
8. Always follow up your graph with a written description.

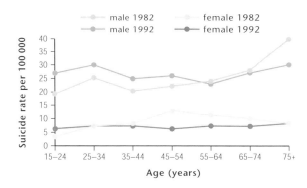

Fig. 4.4 A comparison of suicide rates in Australia for males and females in 1982 and 1992. The rate of suicide has increased for young people (aged 15–24), especially for young males. In contrast, the rate of suicide for the older groups has decreased

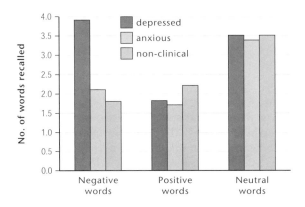

Fig. 4.5 When depressed subjects are shown a series of words, they recall more negative words than do anxious or non-clinical subjects, even though there is no difference in general memory ability on neutral words

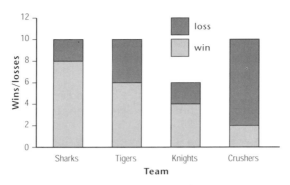

Fig. 4.6 A segmented bar graph is one way of representing the relationship between two categorical relationships, such as this one showing the number of wins and losses of some major Australian Rugby League teams

Bar graphs are used for categorical data, for example, normals, anxious, depressive. Histograms are used when there is a relation between the levels of the independent variable (i.e. the *x*-axis). For example, age groups, such as young, middle and old or 20–24 years, 25–29 years, 30–34 years, may be represented by a histogram but midpoints are used for the data on the ordinate (i.e. the midpoint of each group, 22 years, 27 years, etc.). Line graphs are used for ratio or interval data. Always use a ruler to connect the various data points. You may have been taught to smooth out your line but this is not done in Psychology.

Don't use pie graphs unless you are asked to; use histograms or bar graphs instead. Many computer programs offer three-dimensional bar graphs. Don't use them. They might look sophisticated but that is the problem. Graphs are meant to present information simply, so keep your graphs simple. The same rule applies to the use of colour. Use black and white, then if you need to use grey, but avoid the use of patterns.

4.6.3 Statistics

You may not have to write up statistical expressions in your introductory year in Psychology. Nevertheless, they also have conventions of expression. The following are some example you might come across.

Perhaps you are asked to compute a *t*-test. You may do this by hand or with the aid of computer software. It is easy to get involved with the analysis and forget that the results must be presented properly. Application 2.7 (p. P1.53) in Bond and McConkey (2000) provides a step-by-step guide to the calculations of a *t*-test. For the example given, the result is a *t* value of 1.43 and the *df* is 28. The correct way to write up this information is like this:

$$t(28) = 1.43, \textit{ns} \text{ or } t(28) = 1.43, p > 0.05$$

Note that t is italicised, the degrees of freedom (df) are in brackets, then the value of t, then finally a statement about the value of t. Here t is not significant, which is represented by ns. Had t been significant, it would be because it exceeds a critical value for its degrees of freedom (see Chapter 2 Bond & McConkey, 2000). Suppose that t has the value of 2.23 with 28 degrees of freedom. Under these circumstances one would write:

$$t(28) = 2.23, p < 0.05$$

Or, perhaps, since we can use computers to accurately assess the probability that t has such a value:

$$t(28) = 2.23, p < 0.04$$

because the actual probability for $t(28) = 2.23$ is $p = 0.033\ 943$ and we round up and use the less than sign to summarise the statistic.

Writing up statistics is not just a matter of setting them out as above. You need to set them within the context of writing a written description of your findings. Your written interpretation of your results is the most important part. As with tables and graphs, students often do all the work producing the statistics only to omit writing about what they have produced. Thus, you need to write a statement like:

Males ($\bar{X} = 24.5, SD = 4.5$) were not found to differ significantly from females ($\bar{X} = 21.3, SD = 7.8$) on the dependent measure of the number of cigarettes smoked, $t(28) = 1.43, ns$.

Or:

Male undergraduates ($\bar{X} = 24.5, SD = 4.5$) were found to differ significantly from female undergraduates ($\bar{X} = 21.3, SD = 7.8$) in the number of cigarettes smoked, $t(28) = 2.23, p < 0.05$.

Points to note

- Generally, only round to two decimal places.
- It is not necessary to include a zero before the decimal place (i.e. $p < .001$ or $p < 0.001$).
- Always place a space before and after the operators such as +, =, <, >.

Other common statistics

Table 4.1 Common statistics used

Statistic	General formula	Example
Mean	$\bar{X}$ = {value}	$\bar{X}$ = 24.5
Standard deviation	SD = {value}	SD = 12.2
t-test	$t(df)$ = {value}, probability, < {value}	$t(28)$ = 2.23, $p < 0.05$
Correlation	$r(df)$ = {value}, probability, < {value}	$r(24)$ = 0.43, $p < 0.05$
Chi-square	Chi-square (df, total sample size = {value}) = = {value}, probability, < {value}	χ^2 (4, N = 234) = 13.31, $p < 0.01$

4.6.4 Common abbreviations used in report writing

Table 4.2 lists some common abbreviations used in report writing. This list is not exhaustive; there are many others that psychologists might use in their investigations. You should consult your tutor or the APA Manual for others. One rule always applies: be consistent! Once you adopt an abbreviation, use the same one throughout your report.

Points to note

• Do not represent plurals. It may seem odd that 30 km means 30 kilometres and that 12 cm means 12 centimetres but it's not correct to write 30 kms or 12 cms.

4.7 The discussion

Always begin your discussion with a brief review of your hypothesis or set of hypotheses. You don't need to repeat them exactly as you did in your initial statement at the end of the introduction. Just restate them with sufficient clarity to remind the reader of the purpose of your experiment or investigation.

Your discussion states the importance of *your* study. The discussion section focuses exclusively on what you have found in your research, what theoretical explanation can be given to your results and what the significance of this material is for further research or application. You may need to discuss your findings against material you have already introduced but you should find yourself defining terms or introducing the findings of studies that are similar to those that you produced. Try not to introduce new material here unless that material explains something significant about your results or develops a discussion on where the findings of this sort of research should be applied. Place all introductory material in your introduction.

Table 4.2 Common abbreviations and symbols used within laboratory reports

Units and measures	Symbols	Units and measures	Symbols
centimetre	cm	year	yr
decibel	dB	ohm	Ω
degrees per second	deg/s	analysis of variance	ANOVA
degree Fahrenheit	°F	frequency	f
gram	g	mean square	$\bar{X}^2$
hour	hr	number in subsample	n
hertz	Hz	total sample	N
intelligence quotient	IQ	not significant	ns
kilogram	kg	probability	p
kilometre	km	percentage or percentile	P
kilometres per hour	kph	product moment correlation coefficient	r
litre	L	standard deviation	SD
metre	m	standard error	SE
area	m^2	sum of squares	SS
speed	m/s	value of t-test	t
milligram	mg	horizontal axis (in graph)	x
minute	min	vertical axis (in graph)	y
millilitre	mL	standard score	z
newton	N	increment of change	Δ
second	s	sum	Σ
volt	V	chi-square	χ^2
watt	W		

A good discussion will lead to a paragraph that states what still needs to be explained or researched. Do not only include a statement that further research is needed. The discussion should mention some useful application of the material evaluated and the conclusions that can be drawn from the data you have gathered. This may be stated as if things had been idealised and all the research has turned out perfectly because you will go on to discuss the limitation of your particular research. For example, you might write:

The data indicate that performance at secondary school is not highly correlated with success in first year Psychology. A theoretical explanation for this is that there is a unique combination of skills required for success in Psychology. Further research might examine the relationship between courses at university level that are taught at secondary school to determine whether, for example, success in English at high school is related to success in first year university English courses.

The applications you might discuss would consider whether schools should prepare those people who are interested in studying Psychology.

■

> I have not failed. I've just found 10 000 ways that won't work.
> *Thomas Edison*

The limitations of your research results need to be declared. Often this section will include a statement about the limited sample size, the way you selected participants and the nature of your data analysis.

Examples of possible limitations on your studies include:

1. sample size (laboratory exercises generally rely on only a few participants)
2. the selection of the sample (i.e. your fellow students)
3. cultural biases
4. educational biases (students are not necessarily representative of the wider population)
5. distractions in the laboratory (especially when using animals).

Discussion	Grading
Discussion does not relate to research conducted	D
Conclusions are drawn from the results	C/D
Conclusions are drawn from the results and explained in contrast to previous research and theory	B/A
Conclusions are drawn from the results and explained in contrast to previous research and theory. The limitations of the research are evaluated, practical outcomes of the research are considered	A/A+

4.8 The abstract

You may be asked to provide an abstract. The abstract is not really a part of your research report; it's an executive summary. Normally, an abstract is included in research reports so that the abstract can be indexed on electronic databases. It provides a summary of the research so that others can read quickly what the research is about and decide its usefulness for their purposes. The abstract is a short (less than 200 words) summary explaining what is done in the research and what conclusions are reached. The abstract is not an introduction and its contents should not be relied on in the report. You might imagine that you have written a postcard to a friend or relative and explained what you did in your laboratory exercise. If you wrote a short postcard in formal language and captured all the key points of what you did, how you did it and what conclusion you discovered, then you have the idea.

Points to note

- You may use abbreviations in abstracts when they have a clear meaning.
- Use numbers instead of spelling them out.
- Do not cite the research of others unless the study demands such, as would occur if you were replicating some research. You should then cite the entire reference in the abstract.
- The abstract should be concise, complete, matter-of-fact and direct.
- Explain what you did in the past tense and what your discussion is about in the present tense.

4.9 Things to avoid

The same things to avoid in essay writing apply with research report writing (see Chapter 3). Below are some common mistakes particular to research reports that you should consider.

■

> I can write better than anybody who can write faster, and I can write faster than anybody who can write better.
>
> *A. J. Liebling*

4.9.1 The word 'significantly'

Since social scientists use the word 'significant' to mean something quite mathematical, you need to be very careful how you use it in your report write. For example, in an essay it's fine to say 'It is significant that the argument is limited to Americans because the research probably does not apply to other cultural contexts'. In a research report you may run into difficulty with the expression. For example, the claim, 'There are significant differences between American and Australian cultures', may be interpreted as a general claim that Australians are not quite like Americans or it could mean that the data you collected indicate some difference between an American sample and an Australian sample. The way to avoid the ambiguity is to use 'significant' only in its mathematical sense.

4.9.2 Over-reporting and over-reporting statistics

Most studies do not report all the results they find. Researchers select those important findings that are central to the question they address in the report. This approach is sensible in hindsight but it is one of the most difficult aspects of report writing. The problem arises because a lot of effort goes into analysing data and producing graphs and tables. There is also a pressure to be precise. A symptom of these concerns is the over-reporting of data. People often get caught up with percentages and start to report even very tiny percentages. On a Likert scale you may get responses such as:

Strongly disagree	2%
Disagree	2%
Don't know	15%
Agree	75%
Strongly agree	6%

The temptation is to explain the data by discussing each set of responses but it is unnecessary. The simplest way is to say this is 'Most people (81%) agree or strongly agree with the question that …'. The rest can be left out.

The same thinking applies with the inclusion of tables and graphs. People with some knowledge of their computer's functionality for producing graphs often get carried away and present three or four graphs when one would do. If you can leave a table or graph out then do so. However, the issue is one of balance. If you find yourself writing out lengthy explanations of the findings, then consider a graph or table. The essential rule is to include only what is necessary, and no more!

4.9.3 Correlation and causation

When writing up your report you will need to be careful about the expressions you use that might commit the fallacy that correlation implies causation. Words and expressions such as 'because', 'thus', 'therefore', 'due to' and 'prove' can be strong when talking about research findings. Two things may be correlated because of a common cause. For example, the height of schoolchildren and their age are correlated: here the cause is growth or maturation. Obviously, though, height does not cause age. Less obviously, age does not cause height. Take another example: the number of cars on the highway might well be related to the number of deaths by car accidents but the fact that traffic density and accident fatalities are correlated does not mean that traffic density causes fatal accidents. It might be that people are in more of a hurry at times of high traffic density or simply that the constant rate of accidents is proportional to the number of people on the road. It might be that as the number of people on the road happens to increase, so too do accidents. To put the point bluntly, it would be equally valid to argue that traffic fatalities cause traffic density, which is just absurd.

A correlation is just an observation that two things seem to occur together. They may occur together accidentally, through the influence of a third variable or because one variable causes the other. You must be sensitive to these possibilities. It is wrong to dismiss a correlation as being nothing more than a correlation and therefore not indicative of something causal. It is also wrong to assume causality when none exists. So when considering correlation, always think about the three possibilities:

1. A causes B: traffic density causes accidents
2. C causes A and B: people are less attentive at rush hour and therefore have more accidents.
3. A and B occur together accidentally: as there are more cars on the road, there are more accidents.

4.10 The research report checklist

Research report checklist

	Yes	No
1. The subjects/participants are described.	❏	❏
2. A written description of the key results accompanies all graphs and tables.	❏	❏
3. The introduction develops a discussion of why this research is needed.	❏	❏
4. The hypothesis is a written statement that outlines what is tested in the research.	❏	❏
5. The conclusion is concise but not definitive.	❏	❏
6. The discussion section has a paragraph outlining the limitations of the research.	❏	❏
7. The report outlines its reasoning in the 'signposting paragraph'.	❏	❏
8. The key terms were defined in a paragraph that evaluated several definitions.	❏	❏
9. A variety of referencing techniques are developed, such as listing, pointing and citing.	❏	❏
10. All quotations are evaluated and critically appraised.	❏	❏
11. The conclusion recognises the limitations of the research.	❏	❏
12. All references are listed in the references section.	❏	❏
13. Only the references actually referred to in the essay are in the references section.	❏	❏
14. The essay has a wide margin for the marker's comments.	❏	❏
15. Your name/student number appears on the front page.	❏	❏
16. The report has page numbers.	❏	❏
17. The headings are in a simple format and do not alter the typeface (see p. 41)	❏	❏
18. There are no bullet points or lists of points, even in the methods and results sections.	❏	❏
19. The abstract is 100–150 words.	❏	❏
20. Each paragraph attempts to address a single issue or theme.	❏	❏
21. The short paragraph isn't used at any point other that to outline the hypothesis.	❏	❏
22. The writing is formal.	❏	❏
23. The references are all in APA style.	❏	❏
24. The references section is not labelled 'bibliography'.	❏	❏
25. There are no contractions, such as wouldn't or can't.	❏	❏
26. The report is evenly balanced in its critique of the evidence.	❏	❏
27. The report is no more than ± 5–10% of the word limit.	❏	❏
28. Past research is summarised in the introduction and this leads to a statement about the aim of the present research.	❏	❏
29. The practical applications of this knowledge, evidence or argument are presented in the discussion section.	❏	❏
30. I have not used sexist language or represented the work of others as my own.	❏	❏

4.11 Frequently asked questions

What's the difference between a figure and a table?

Figures are illustrations and tables present data. Figures may represent diagrams, models or graphs for illustrative purposes whereas tables present information from which conclusions may be drawn. In practical terms, tables are retyped by the typesetter and figures are photographed. When you are writing up your report, your graphs will be figures and your tables will be tables.

What does $p < 0.05$ mean?

Chapter 2 in Bond and McConkey 2000 explains critical values. Here, the discussion is restricted to how to write out these values. In brief, though, the value $p < 0.05$ means that there are less than five chances in 100 that the samples you selected (i.e. the values you obtained for the two groups) were drawn from the same population.

What tense should be used?

With essay writing you are trying to convince someone of an argument, your case or your evaluation of research. This is best achieved in the present tense: for example, 'This argument establishes ...'. In a research report you are telling a story about events that occurred in the past, about what you found out, about the implications of that work. Generally, you will cast your report in the past tense. For example, in your discussion, you may write, 'This investigation established that ...'. However, in your results section you will generally use the present tense: 'These data establish that x is independent of y ...'. Your abstract combines tenses. You will report what you did in the past tense and what the report argues in the present tense. A rule of thumb to remember is: 'respondents were/data are' (Backstrom & Hursh-Cesar, 1981). You might rephrase this to: 'what was done/this is the result'.

CHAPTER 5
APPRAISING THEORY
AND ARGUMENTS

OVERVIEW

5.1 How do theories function?
5.2 The prime directive
5.3 How to be critical effectively
5.4 Developing your argument
5.5 Avoiding fallacies
5.6 How to avoid fallacies

Some parts of Psychology are dense with theoretical controversies. For example, the 'big' nature versus nurture question arises within Developmental Psychology. Other areas seem comparatively lacking in broad theories and controversy, for example, Physiological Psychology. There are many 'little' theories in Social and Cognitive Psychology, such as theories of social bias and social cognition. There are also grand theories, such as psychoanalytic theory, and theoretical divides, such as those that inform our understanding of motivation—drive theories versus incentive theories. There are also philosophical perspectives that divide Psychology, such as reductionism and constructionism. As there are so many theories, almost all psychologists will regard themselves as theoreticians, especially when they are confronted with the argument that Psychology should have specialised theoreticians (see Slife & Williams, 1997). For now, it is best to say that you will need to learn a lot of theories and, in doing so, evaluate their usefulness in some manner.

■

Eagles may soar, but weasels don't get sucked into jet engines.
John Benfield

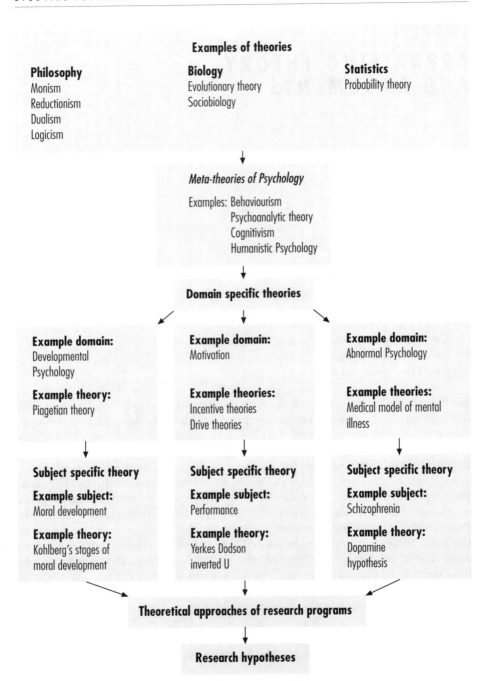

Examples of theories

Philosophy
Monism
Reductionism
Dualism
Logicism

Biology
Evolutionary theory
Sociobiology

Statistics
Probability theory

Meta-theories of Psychology

Examples: Behaviourism
Psychoanalytic theory
Cognitivism
Humanistic Psychology

Domain specific theories

Example domain:
Developmental
Psychology

Example theory:
Piagetian theory

Example domain:
Motivation

Example theories:
Incentive theories
Drive theories

Example domain:
Abnormal Psychology

Example theories:
Medical model of mental
illness

Subject specific theory

Example subject:
Moral development

Example theory:
Kohlberg's stages of
moral development

Subject specific theory

Example subject:
Performance

Example theory:
Yerkes Dodson
inverted U

Subject specific theory

Example subject:
Schizophrenia

Example theory:
Dopamine
hypothesis

Theoretical approaches of research programs

Research hypotheses

Fig. 5.1 Theories from outside Psychology

The notion of how theories function, what sort of structure they have, and how they are developed, confirmed and rejected is probably best left to the branch of philosophy called the Philosophy of Science. However, some simplification of the issues might help. You need to understand some general principles for assessing theories and presenting your argument. From these simplifications we can discuss how to critically appraise the arguments that comprise a theory and how to structure your own arguments. The three below will serve as a start.

5.1 How do theories function?

1. Theories organise a body of knowledge.
2. Theories help develop research and define what research is acceptable.
3. Theories in Psychology explain research findings concerning behaviour and experience.

One thing we can recognise is that theories are intimately related to evidence. Just as a lawyer's case is about material facts, so too, theories in Psychology are about psychological facts. Theories are meant to place facts together into a coherent picture of what actually occurs, develop a perspective on what facts still need to be explained and explain what occurs—just like the mystery of a crime.

Thus, theories are arguments about facts. The words 'theory' and 'argument' are interwoven around evidence. To develop the argument of an essay is to adopt a theory. To adopt a theory is to adopt an argument about evidence. We don't have the privilege of having our case assigned to us as a lawyer does. We need to know how to appraise theories and adopt the best argument.

5.2 The prime directive

All theories in Psychology are controversial and can be defended by arguments of increasing complexity. Academics who develop theories rarely concede their position: they may stubbornly develop clever arguments against the development of clever arguments to criticise their work. Sometimes this defence involves sophisticated attacks on the methodologies used as evidence in the critiques of the theory—in the kind of 'nice try but it's not good enough' way. It is worth restating that nearly all psychologists claim to be theoreticians. It is also worth remembering, despite the resistance, that some of the best theories have been proven wrong.

■

> We shall not cease from exploration, and the end of all our exploring will be to arrive where we started and know the place for the first time.   *T. S. Eliot*

You should keep these points in mind when you evaluate any theory. It is unlikely that you will be able to reach a firm conclusion regarding the adequacy of a theoretical position. You will still need to argue to reach a conclusion but you won't ever achieve a definitive answer. Thus, the prime rule when writing about a theoretical position or presenting a theoretical critique is: you will be graded on the quality of your argument, not whether you reach the 'right' conclusion!

5.3 How to be critical effectively

Bond and McConkey (2000) presents you with many theories and develops an understanding of their usefulness by presenting research that has been conducted to develop, support or challenge the theory. The textbook's approach to dealing with theory is probably the best way to proceed with assessing any theoretical claim, whether it is a grand theory of Psychology or a little theory. Even a broad hypothesis that makes some claim about the nature of a particular set of behaviours is a type of theory and can be assessed this way. By listing out those things that do not seem to accord with a general position, you acquire an evidential challenge to a theoretical claim, even if you concede the evidence supports the theory.

5.3.1 A general strategy for approaching theory

The general approach to theory appraisal is listed in a formula-like fashion in the six points below. A similar strategy was adopted for essay writing. This is the basic formula, but again, it's not the only way, nor is it necessarily the best.
   A basic approach to the consideration of theory is:

1. Describe the theoretical position.
2. Define the key terms by quoting sources directly.
3. Provide the evidential counter examples: research that the theory cannot explain or does not explain well.
4. Consider the limitations to your challenge: what does the theory still explain very well?
5. Consider alternative theories and evaluate whether they explain things as well or better.
6. Consider what sort of research would solve the issue or what practical outcome there is if the issues are resolved.

This outline is simply a brief version of the essay formula in Chapter 3. The formula is a type of argument—again that is why it has to be adjusted and improved—but serves as a general scaffolding for you to develop your own argument.

■

> The reasonable man adapts himself to the world; the unreasonable one persists in trying to adapt the world to himself. Therefore, all progress depends on the unreasonable man.
>
> *George Bernard Shaw*

5.3.2 Describing the theoretical position

A good piece of advice comes from Kahneman and Tversky (1996), who respond to an attack on their own theoretical developments by stating:

> It is always useful to remember that the refutation of a caricature can be no more than a caricature of refutation. (p. 584)

What this means is if you do not know the theory well and fail to represent its components correctly, then you cannot criticise it well. If you misrepresent a crucial element of a theory, you set up the possibility of arguing against what philosophers call the 'straw man' (or 'straw person', if you prefer). The notion of a straw man is that a weak description of the theory can be easily defeated with some evidential counter example, whereas a stronger description of the theory would not be defeated by the argument. Sometimes writers weaken theories unintentionally; sometimes they fail to be charitable enough to the theoretical position to give it a good hearing before launching into their critique.

For example, it is commonplace to link Piaget's theory of cognitive development to the ages of children. Suppose someone declares that children of age 3 are in the preoperational stage. Then, by demonstrating that children of age 3 have a more sophisticated level of thinking than that described in Piaget's theory (i.e. can perform a concrete operation), the theory of cognitive development is undermined. But a fallacy is committed. Piaget explicitly declared that the stages he proposed were not age related. So the supposed criticism fails to represent his theory accurately and ignores the crucial point that children are meant to progress through the stages in a specified sequence and that this sequence is incidentally related to their age. The risk you run in presenting a straw man is that you fail to appreciate the good points of a theory (see below for more examples). In the example given, this means understanding the sequence of development and the types of mechanism that allow the advance from one stage to the next.

5.3.3 How to avoid the 'straw man'

Quote an original source

Remember the advice for essay writing that you should only quote what you disagree with. To avoid the straw man is exactly why you should quote what you disagree with. You should not fall into the trap of the straw man if you faithfully interpret a claim, quote it and then state the point of disagreement. It is hard to misrepresent a position that is derived directly from the original source. Remember, however, to only quote the part you disagree with. It is not a good strategy to quote large chunks of a theoretical position just to represent it accurately. Part of your assessment will be based on how well you can represent the position in your own words.

Don't rely solely on someone else's description of a theoretical position

You may not read the original work of a theoretician, especially at an introductory level, but do not limit yourself to one description of a theory. This is especially true if that description leads to some criticism. Find at least two or three perspectives on the position. You can do this by examining texts and general works that will outline the material in general and noting any discrepancies between the accounts.

5.4 Developing your argument

5.4.1 What is an argument?

There is no need to get philosophical about this. You have opinions and you have argued for a whole range of things before you ever studied Psychology. You will have tried to persuade someone else to do something for you, considered what the best political party is, decided whether it's a good idea to study Psychology or some alternative and so on. To raise an argument is part of everyday life. To raise an argument in Psychology is not. The difference is more in the manner of presentation than the substance of the argument. You know already that the evidence you work with is the research and theories of Psychology. You also know there are a lot of rules for how to write your argument to hold the reader's (the marker of your essay) attention.

■

Change your thoughts and you change your world.
Norman Vincent Peale

Recall our legal analogy developed in Chapter 3. Your argument against a theory is much like arguing against what the opposition states is its case. Its case is a theory of the events leading to the crime. Your theory of events needs to be seen as a better theory, a more accurate theory, or at least, a good case. Your argument might be that the case isn't made or you might present (not create) a better theory of events. Beyond this analogy, it's up to you how you create an argument. Below, however, are some examples of strategies and things to avoid that you should consider carefully.

5.4.2 Some tips on creating an argument

- Avoid choosing a topic that you feel strongly about. Part of your grading is given to your ability to research out facts and form the argument. This task is made much more difficult if you have a preconceived idea about the facts or a theory that you particularly like.
- Read the work of others for their arguments. You don't need to develop a novel argument; you need to develop a well-reasoned argument that is arranged in a novel way. Presenting someone else's argument is fine provided you develop the case by presenting evidence that develops into an essay that demonstrates your involvement. You should not stand aside and let others do all the work by presenting their arguments. Remember to reference the ideas of those that you are representing.
- Try not to be too forceful with your argument. It's sufficient, and normally preferred, to raise some doubt about the adequacy of competing arguments.
- Do not assume that a criticism of a theory is adequate simply because some other researcher has presented it. Always evaluate the argument and the soundness of the evidential support for the criticism. A good strategy for the development of an argument is to defend against a criticism presented by someone else (see below).
- Avoid attacking the logic of a theory. This is because it is extremely difficult to pull off and will generally place your argument in the realm of philosophy, not Psychology, so you are unlikely to score well with it, even if it is a good argument. If you can, point to logical errors and derive their consequences.
- Defend the weak position. Playing devil's advocate and defending an argument that appears weak is often a good way to develop a novel essay. You must not try to defend the argument against good criticism or ignore the weight of evidence against the view you are defending. However, if you focus on what remains after the attacks have been made, the range of arguments that are left might surprise you. Further, you will be forced to state the theory, the criticism and the limitations of the criticisms, so you will cover all the bases and score reasonably well. For example:

> Piaget's theory of cognitive development has sustained decades of criticism and perhaps the prevailing opinion is that there are better theories now. Still, Piaget's theory can be credited for its ability to sustain decades of criticism, initiate inquiry into the processes of the developing mind, coincide with the behaviourist doctrines that dominated Psychology and lead to Kolhberg's theorising about moral development.

- Use signposts to define your argument. These signposts define *your* perspective. It's worth reiterating that you should not use personal pronouns in your essay and say such things as 'I will argue ...' or 'My argument is ...'. When people write 'Nonetheless, the material has not considered ...', they are indicating their contribution to the argument and signposting this to the reader. Here are a few examples and what they mean:
  - 'Nonetheless ...': Author accepts the argument presented previously but will outline some limitation.
  - 'Nevertheless ...': Author accepts the argument presented previously but that argument has an inherent limitation.
  - 'Notwithstanding ...': The argument is accepted. Author goes on to explain some new aspect of the argument.
  - 'However ...': Author disagrees with the argument and will state the reason.
  - 'Given the ...': Author will continue with the argument presented and show it's limitations or lead it to a logical absurdity.
  - 'Albeit ...': Same as 'given the'.
  - 'Further/Furthermore ...': In addition to the previously stated argument.

5.4.3 There is no argument!

Occasionally essay topics and research reports seem to be about topics in which you have no argument to address. Essay questions that ask you to *describe* some body of knowledge are often more difficult for students than those that introduce some controversy or theoretical claim. You will often have this difficulty with an essay in Physiological Psychology. A series of mistakes derives from the inability to form an argument because the essay is about a series of factual claims. The most common temptation is to paraphrase the work in the text and simply add an introduction. You will be able to recognise this difficulty in advance because you won't be able to write down any reasonable conclusion and you will find the essay tedious to research and write. These essays become tedious and difficult to read, and generally attract poor grades.

Solutions

An essay is always an argument! If there is no way to develop the argument based on the content of the essay, then the production of your essay is the argument. Instead of your argument being about some theory or set of research, your argument is, 'this presentation is a really good way to understand these facts'. Any one of the following strategies can be used to overcome the problem.

1. Develop one metaphor or analogy and use it throughout to describe the undisputed facts.

Example: Brain function can be compared to a telephone network, where the peripheral nervous system is the incoming calls and the thalamus is the exchange.

2. Develop an argument based on the applications of the information that is too factually dense to critique. Your essay question, then, is 'Given facts A, B, C we can do X and Y, but not Z'. This might be put as a question, 'What are the limitations of the knowledge we have acquired?'

Example: Knowledge of brain structures allows us to develop research focusing on particular areas and an understanding of the functional loss due to injury but has not revealed the nature of consciousness.

3. Explain the relevant historical context in which the information that is now undisputed was developed.

Example: René Descartes thought that the pineal gland was the link between consciousness and physiology but we now know that this is not true and now believe that there is no particular area of the brain that serves as a bridge between consciousness and physiology.

4. Describe the techniques used to develop information that seems un-controversial.

Example: PET, MRI and EEG all function differently to reveal different aspects of brain structure and provide different information about brain function.

5.5 Avoiding fallacies

5.5.1 Fallacies

A fallacy is sometimes thought to be any type of illogical argument or false reasoning. But this is far too broad to be useful. When you consider that there are rules for arguments you will find a convenient meaning to the notion of a fallacy. A fallacy is simply a violation of the rules for argumentation. Many different fallacies are presented below, some with more than one type. The classification of fallacies used derives from a philosophical outline, first proposed by Aristotle, but in the modern context of Psychology. There are two divisions: fallacies due to reasoning and fallacies due to language. The classification here is certainly not the only way to order fallacies of reasoning, nor is it necessarily complete, but the outlines and examples should be helpful.

Fallacies are not technicalities of philosophy. You can spot illogical reasoning in the arguments of others—particularly when they lead to a clear contradiction. More importantly, others can spot fallacious reasoning in the arguments you develop. This is true whether or not they know the name of the fallacy as it might be classified in philosophy. However, while these are types of arguments you should avoid, being familiar with them will allow you to spot them in the arguments in material you read. You will find fallacies in the writings of the materials you read as they are over 2000 years old and are unlikely to disappear in modern writing just because we can name them.

5.5.2 Fallacies due to reasoning

The fallacy of accident

This fallacy consists of confusing an unessential difference with an essential difference or when confusing an unessential resemblance with an essential resemblance. It is surprisingly easy to do. Here is an example:

> Is Psychology different from physics? Yes!
> Is physics a science? Yes!
> Then, since Psychology is different from physics, Psychology is not a
> science.

It is important to ask whether Psychology is different from physics in some material way. Clearly, physics is different from Psychology in terms of its subject matter, and the methods that are used to study that subject matter are different. But are these differences significant? Because we know that there are other sciences that do not study the same thing as physics, for example, chemistry, we know the subject matter is not material to whether a subject is a science. However, perhaps the differences between the methods of physics and the methods of Psychology are sufficient that the former is a science and the latter not? If you believe this, you need to state explicitly what those differences are to avoid the fallacy.

Ignoring the qualification and overstating the case: converse of the fallacy of accident (a dicto secundum quid ad dictum simpliciter)

This fallacy consists in assuming that something that is true in some special circumstances will hold true without restriction or as a general rule. In Psychology, we constantly battle against committing this fallacy because we infer from surveys, experiments and observation information to general points about human behaviour. Psychology is often cynically accused of being the study of first year Psychology students, because often enough, first year Psychology students are the most convenient sample of people to study. Here is an example:

> Students are similar to all other people.
> People are found to have an average IQ of 100.
> Students have an average IQ of 100.

Students are often used as subjects because sometimes they will not differ from other people in the community generally. But a group of university students is very unlikely to have an average IQ of 100. So, be careful when you are reasoning from your evidence to a wider conclusion about people, or the nature of a problem in Psychology.

Ignorance of the nature of refutation (ignoratio elenchi)

For an argument to be effective it must not only reason to an acceptable conclusion; the conclusion reached should address the point of concern. Whenever students get a comment 'did not address the question', they feel a bit cheated. Surely it's a great essay, well reasoned, well written and so on? Yes, but did it address the question? If you argue against a particular proposition, you must ensure that your conclusion is contrary to the alternative conclusion. The alternative you present must be the opposite of the assertion challenged, not something similar, and not something altogether unrelated to the position you are attacking. There are five divisions of this fallacy; the first is the most important.

1 Proving the wrong point

If you were to argue that deception is a necessary part of psychological experimentation, it would be no good to reach the conclusion that experimentation has no place in modern Psychology. Even if you concede that experimentation in the laboratory is not the ideal way to proceed with Social Psychology, you need not concede that deception is not a useful component to social psychological experimentation. You can avoid the fallacy by being deliberate in your attempts to outline the positions that you are arguing against. As mentioned above, the fallacy of the straw man is one example of this type of error because the straw man is presented as an answer to the question instead of addressing the question.

2 Attacking the person (argumentum ad hominem)

The *ad hominem* is the argument that attacks the person, rather than the argument the person presents. The legal analogy is appropriate here. Instead of defending the client by pointing to facts and evidence, the lawyer can use the strategy of attacking the character of the witnesses. Remember, it's always an issue of the credibility of the research or the usefulness of the argument, not the quality of the character who performs the research. Use of the *ad hominem* falls within this classification of fallacies because, like proving the wrong point, it fails to address the argument.

It is rare that students will invoke an attack on the person because they soon recognise that it is the argument that they are concerned with, not the person who said it. Still, in a milder form, some people will argue, for example: 'Piaget's theory was once popular but modern concern is with the constructionist approach of Vygotsky and others'. You should see this statement is insufficient in itself (in fact it commits several fallacies). A reason needs to be given why it is that

Vygotsky's theory has attracted modern concern, what criticisms are levelled at Piaget's theory and so on.

3 Emotive arguments (*argumentum ad populum*)

'Everyone will agree that it's wrong to deceive participants about the nature of the research project.'

Such a statement is misguided. The point of academic arguments is to stand aside from what people might agree with and evaluate objectively. Even the worst positions must be critically appraised rather than condemned without inspection. You must consider possibilities and evidence and avoid following or producing arguments that are based in the appeal to emotive issues.

4 Appeals to an authority (*argumentum ad verecundiam*)

This fallacy is an appeal to authority instead of to reason. There is no necessary connection between who says a statement and its truthfulness or validity. We are particularly prone to this fallacy in Psychology because sometimes facts get confused with reasons. The worst form of this fallacy is when we say, for example: 'Professor J. Blithe argues ...'. As you know already, appealing to researchers or their titles is something to be avoided (see p. 38). An unevaluated quotation also commits this fallacy (see p. 32).

5 The fallacy of the consequent

This is also known as the *non sequitur* and affirming the consequent. The converse fallacy is called denial of the antecedent. This is an especially important set of fallacies for social scientists because we deal with facts and build arguments and theories based on a series of facts derived from research. We are different from philosophers who deal with these fallacies with different assumptions. Here is an example:

'If Psychology is a science, then psychologists use experiments to determine facts.'

The sentence or meaning that comes before 'If" is called the antecedent. The rest of the sentence that follows 'then' is called the consequent. There is nothing wrong with this statement as it's presented. Psychologists do perform experiments and all sciences perform experiments of one form or other. You may validly argue these points:

1. Psychology is a science, therefore it will involve experiments. (affirming the antecedent)
2. Psychology does not involve experiments, therefore Psychology is not a science. (denying the consequent)

However, it is invalid, that is, it is a fallacy, to argue either of the following:

3. Psychology performs experiments, therefore Psychology is a science. (affirming the consequence)
4. Psychology is not a science; therefore Psychology does not involve experiments. (deny the antecedent)

Remember, you might experiment with your video cassette recorder (VCR) to program it properly but that does not define getting your VCR to work as a science (though it ought to be!). Even if science involves experimentation, there are instances of experimentation that are not scientific and scientific enterprises that do not involve experimentation.

Begging the question (petitio principii)

There are five forms of this fallacy. The general form of the mistake can be characterised as the tendency to assert in one's argument the conclusion that one is intending to reach. It is difficult to commit some forms of this fallacy unless there is some sort of confusion in the writing. However, it is quite common for students to do this by asserting something is self-evident or truthful when it is the very topic of their essay. The third example is the most important for you to grasp. Let us continue with the example question: 'Is Psychology a science?'.

1 Assume the proposition to be proved

The first way to beg the question is to assume a conclusion for the very point in question. You might do this by simply ignoring the issue and starting off your essay defining Psychology as 'the scientific study of the human mind and its functions, especially those affecting behaviour (Allen, 1990). This definition is from *The concise Oxford dictionary of current English*, and use of a dictionary definition in your concept definition paragraph means you risk begging the question. An essay that commits this fallacy would then continue to discuss what Psychology studies scientifically. The real problem comes at the end when the writer tries to conclude. Such writers will generally just restate that Psychology is an interesting science full of wonderful ideas and many areas of research. It may be a good essay but it could never score more than a C grade simply because it has failed to address the question by assuming an adequate answer at the outset.

2 Assuming the general case

If you take for granted the general case of which the question of interest can be derived, you beg the question of whether the general case is true. You can do this by asserting that all social sciences are scientific, or not, and then declaring that Psychology is a social science. Writers who assert that 'all deception is wrong' and then declare that deception in social psychological research is wrong commit the fallacy of begging the question whether it is indeed true that all deception is wrong. After all, we lie about Santa Claus, the surprise party and the coordination of pink and red clothing because to speak truthfully might cause more harm than good.

This problem is very important in Psychology because it is often hard to find a set of self-evident truths from which to begin the argument. With some essay questions the problem is easy to overcome. The fundamental here is research. Begin by presenting the research and build your argument by evaluating how the research supports a position. With other essay questions that are more philosophical (Introductory Psychology essay questions often are, e.g. 'Do IQ test measure intelligence?'), the trick is to recognise that the position you want to start from may be a bit shaky so you will need to explore more than one side of the argument (see below). Thus, instead of assuming things, you raise the concerns, point to the issues and research, and consider the arguments for and against the position. You may never reach a firm conclusion, but then if you don't start out on solid ground, this should be expected.

3 The inductive fallacy (*per enumerationem simplicem*)

Students often write down individual cases, facts or personal experiences that are not research, as if the individual case were sufficient evidence. This occurs because of confusion between presenting evidence to support an argument and presenting examples to illustrate a type of reasoning. In other words, there is confusion between reasoning and arguing about facts. It's often difficult to sort issues of theory from issues of fact because theories function as outlined above— they organise facts and explain evidence.

You may illustrate your claim with some single cases but these will not prove your case. Thus, use anecdotal evidence (the single case) as an illustration for your arguments but do not use it as evidence. Use personal examples sparingly and never use them when psychological research will or should support your reasoning.

4 Begging the question by converse relation

This fallacy is not too difficult to spot. Suppose you say that sociology is less scientific than Psychology, give reasons why and then go on to conclude that Psychology is more scientific than sociology. The comparison may be useful but the question begged is 'what is proved by the comparison?'. You may have established that Psychology is more scientific than sociology but that begs the question of whether *either* Psychology or sociology is a science.

5 The fallacy of many questions

This fallacy consists of requiring a 'yes' or 'no' answer to a question when none is possible. 'Many questions' arise because in forcing an issue into two alternatives, the fallacy disguises the many questions that need to be addressed. When given an essay question like 'Is Psychology a science?', it is impossible to answer the question one way or the other. To even address the question you must first define 'science' and 'Psychology'.

Suppose you decide, after examining what a science is, that only the activity of experimentation is scientific. Then, some parts of Psychology are scientific, specifically those that involve experimentation, such as Neurophysiological Psychology, parts of Cognitive Psychology, and parts of Social Psychology. But, the important question raised in this simple evaluation is whether Neurophysiological Psychology, Social Psychology and Cognitive Psychology characterise Psychology? When you try to define Psychology, you will soon find that not all of Psychology involves experimentation and you will need to consider (ask the many questions) whether these other parts are scientific—Clinical Psychology, Humanistic Psychology, longitudinal studies in Developmental Psychology and so on. Putting the problem the other way around, you might decide that Behaviourist Psychology is really representative of Psychology but then the many questions you would need to answer are whether the methods and thinking of Behaviourist Psychology are truly scientific.

You can spot the fallacy of many questions in essays that reach a definitive conclusion—it is rare to reach a firm conclusion in Psychology because there are normally many assumptions that need to be put to rest before you can even reach a tentative conclusion. Be aware that many of your essay questions will be posed in such a way that you are asked to explore the 'many questions' and that lecturers are fond of presenting essay questions that set you up for this fallacy. If you think you can answer the essay in a word (either yes or no), your task is really to discuss the many questions.

5.5.3 Fallacies of language

Ambiguity of the word (equivocation)

To equivocate is to disguise with ambiguity the clear meaning of an argument. One way to do this is to set out a general principle and then argue a specific case that appears in language to be an example of the general rule but in fact differs in meaning. Here is an example:

> To be awake and alert is to be fully conscious.
> My Parrot is awake and alert.
> My parrot is conscious of its existence.

The first sentence of the argument (the first premise) starts by discussing consciousness in the sense of being awake or not asleep. The second sentence (the minor premise) links being awake with my parrot. The third sentence (the conclusion) discusses consciousness in a different manner. Two different senses of consciousness are discussed and thus the premises have no real relation to the conclusion and commit a fallacy. Here is another example:

> All criminal actions can be overcome by psychologists rehabilitating the individual using behaviour modification.
> Prosecutions for theft are criminal actions.
> Psychologists should rehabilitate prosecutors for theft.

The ambiguity of the word always arises as a confusion of definitions. This is why it is important to define your concepts clearly and keep with them throughout your discussion. Here the ambiguity is caused by the term 'criminal actions'; it needs a clear definition to avoid prosecutions being regarded as criminal actions.

Ambiguity of structure

These fallacies are rare and difficult to conceive without a grammatical error of some form. The fallacy is one in which ambiguity is brought about by the structure of the sentence rather than ambiguity with the meaning of terms.

For example, take the sentence, 'Children with ADHD who have difficulty concentrating have been given Ritalin'. In one sense, the sentence can be interpreted that children who have been given Ritalin have difficulty concentrating. But Ritalin actually improves concentration, thus the fallacy. In its other sense, it means those children with ADHD who have difficult concentrating can be given Ritalin to improve their ability to concentrate. A comma may fix the sentence but it really needs to be rewritten for clarity. The comma would go after the word 'concentrating'. The sentence could be rewritten as 'Ritalin is given to children with ADHD to improve their concentration'.

The fallacy of composition

The fallacy of composition and the fallacy of division (see below) are converse fallacies. The fallacy of composition arises when a term is used to describe a class of things collectively that ought to be described individually. The fallacy of division involves arguing from the fact that something which is true of a general class is true of individuals of that class. The fallacy of division is the more common and more important. Here is an example of the fallacy of composition:

> Psychologists have established that all jurors are prone to errors in judgment.
> Therefore the jury is prone to errors of judgment.

The fallacy occurs if one ignores the fact that a jury is not the same as all the individual members taken collectively. If we simply asked jurors to vote on the outcome of a trial, we would have a valid conclusion. But juries (as opposed to jurors) are a collective of people who interact to form a final judgment of guilt or innocence. So, while jurors may be prone to error, juries may or may not be. At any rate, you cannot declare from a set of jurors what a jury will decide or that the jury is prone to errors of judgment.

The fallacy of division

The fallacy of division is a symptom of forcing an argument to do too much. Here is a typical example:

> People who wear spectacles have a higher IQ on average than any other group of people.

This person wears spectacles.
This person has a higher IQ than others.

This is fairly obviously an error of sorts. We know that an individual may wear glasses and be quite dull—although genius was once thought to be associated with short-sightedness (Ochse, 1990). When we are speaking of individuals, it is often easy to see the error. But when we speak of a subclass of people, it get more confusing. Here is a classic example of the fallacy of division in Psychology:

Minority A's score 10 IQ points lower on average than Europeans. All members of minority A should be given separate, special classes to help them cope with the modern world.

Here is the problem. Suppose it were the true that some group of people scored lower than the average European IQ score, on average. Still, some minority A people will have an IQ score that exceeds the average European score, so there is really no basis to say that all minority A people would benefit from special classes. Some members of the minority group will be exceedingly bright, even if it were true that in general the minority group scores lower on IQ tests.

The fallacy of accent

This fallacy has a modern equivalent expressed from a more ancient version of confusing the written accentuation in Greek. Today it is recognised in the misquotation of others by attributing things to an author that the author did not mean. Here is how it can be done. Suppose the original quotation says 'The public's attitudes toward the mentally ill are that they are dangerous, prone to violence and inclined to criminal behaviour'. Suppose the quotation comes from the Association of Clinical Practitioners. Now the clever but devious writer can claim 'the Association of Clinical Practitioners claims ... the mentally ill are ... dangerous, prone to violence and inclined to criminal behaviour'.

One reason for writing in the page reference for a quotation is that others may check this to assess whether you may have made this sort of error. In this example it is obvious that an error has been committed and you could even reason that such a mistake would need to be intentional. However, the fallacy is easily committed in more subtle ways. This is one reason why you should critically appraise all the material you quote. More importantly, choose quotations that have a clear meaning, try to quote entire sentences and avoid omitting material.

5.6 How to avoid fallacies

Do not ignore contradictory evidence

You must evaluate everything, even the criticisms raised by other people that you want to agree with, because it suits the purpose of your argument. A good argument assesses all the evidence and reaches a conclusion accordingly. If you are inclined to ignore evidence or an argument that seems to have a strong point against the case you are developing, then the best strategy is to refine your conclusions, not to ignore the evidence. Even the best criticisms of the behaviourist doctrine have not been able to dent its superb ability to provide a reasoned set of strategies for reducing phobias. The form of therapy known as systematic desensitisation derives directly from behaviourist principles. Thus, one can always say something about a position that has merit; it would not have been developed if it had no merit.

Check your grammar

Be aware that your grammar can misrepresent your position to your audience. Here is an example of a major headline from a local paper:

> Parctical approach often best when striving to demolish the language barrier (*Hutt News*, Oct. 19, 1999)

Here is an example altered from a real report:

> Enforcement of drink-driving in Wellington has occurred with greater frequency since 1995.

When you think about these two sentences, you realise they are not quite right and not jokes either (although you might wonder about the first). Everyone will write one or two of these accidentally every now and then, particularly the first one. A spell checker will detect the mistake in the first example, but not the mistake in the second. The second example is often overlooked and repeated throughout a report or essay. It's very important that you proofread your work, and better still, get someone else to look at it.

Be honest, critical and open

Fallacies of thought and argument come about when people try too hard to force their reasoning on a particular line. If something doesn't seem quite right it probably isn't quite right. The best solution is to avoid complexity and keep your message simple. Always consider your audience to be charitable but critical. You should be the one controlling the argument, do not assume that a reader (especially the marker) will take control and think too hard about the issues you raise. A reader will generally only make an effort to point out your errors of logic, not the good lines of reasoning you develop. A reader will evaluate the whole of your argument charitably, but will be critical of any errors.

CHAPTER 6
FINDING AND USING RESOURCES

OVERVIEW

6.1   Terminology frustration
6.2   Types of materials
6.3   Lectures
6.4   Frequently asked questions

6.1 Terminology frustration

It takes time to learn the language of Psychology. You may find that terms are confusing. General terms such as 'proposition', 'determinism', 'cognition', 'subjective' and 'empirical' are especially confusing when used in combinations within one sentence. Words such as 'Gestalt', 'behaviourism', 'saturation', 'strabismus' and so on will flummox you at first.

Imagine being in a lecture of first year philosophy that begins:

'Today we are going to examine the empirical verifiability of cognitively significant propositions.'

Imagine further that the lecturer has a combined British *and* Texan accent, performs some hand waving for accentuation and periodically stares vaguely at his left hand. You puzzle on the meaning of the statement for 30 minutes while the lecturer ploughs through two centuries of philosophical thought but are greatly relieved in the tutorial to have another lecturer translate what was said to:

'How we know whether a sentence is true or false.'

You might seriously wonder whether you belong at university. Although such a statement might only be made in a philosophy lecture, psychology lectures can be just as technical.

Complex expressions can be understood, and expressed, in simple ways. It is not wrong to use technical expressions; they allow a fluency in communication between experts. However, when you start out you are not an expert, so you will have to translate many expressions into ideas you can understand.

Often the terminology within books, texts and especially journals is new to us and very confusing, which makes reading the material far from fluent. Unlike lecturers, authors rarely get feedback from students complaining that they don't understand the meaning. All disciplines have their particular terminology, style and forms of expression. The other subjects you take will place a similar demand on you to learn a new jargon. Comprehending the language of a discipline like Psychology will develop over time, with patience. It will take a lot of reading but don't become frustrated with the time it takes or the feeling that you are stumbling through it. Write down the definitions of words you look up. Keep looking them up and writing them down until you know their meaning without looking. Fluency will develop. You wouldn't expect to learn a foreign language immediately, and in a very direct sense, you are being asked to learn a language that will be foreign to you at first.

As an exercise to help you, consider the concept that is defined in a technical sense and compare it to its everyday sense? A word like 'addiction', for example, means something very different in Physiological Psychology from what it does in an everyday context. Write down the technical meaning and the everyday meaning (you might get one from a dictionary if you are stuck). Write down any difference between the definitions.

For example, 'drive' means something different in Psychology from in the dictionary.

- What is the Psychology meaning?
- What is the everyday meaning?
- Any similarity?
- What is the essential difference?

6.2 Types of materials

6.2.1 Special advice

1. Find the section in your library where the Psychology books are held. Normally, it's BF.1. Here you will find most of the books you will need in Psychology in your introductory year. Spend half an hour every now and then browsing over the shelves and looking at the types of books that appear there. ·

   Table 6.1 shows an outline of the usual classification of books in Psychology, which is the US Library of Congress classification system. Not all libraries will adopt this system and some will have newer subsections. Become familiar with your library's system of classification, even if you do this by browsing. Often the library will have a pamphlet that provides exactly this sort of outline. Note, however, that some books relevant to Psychology will be held outside of the main collection of Psychology (e.g. Clinical Psychology books are held along with books on psychiatry and medicine in the classification system outlined below).

Table 6.1   Classifications relevant to Psychology

Classification	Section
General Psychology	BF
Abnormal Psychology	BF173
Psychoanalytic theory	BF173.A2–175
Psychological tests	BF176
Senses and sensation	BF231–299
Cognitive Psychology	BF309–493
Perception	BF311
Learning and conditioning	BF335–337
Memory	BF370–395
Industrial and Applied Psychology	BF481–483
Motivation	BF501–504.3
Emotion	BF511–593
Comparative Psychology	BF660–678
Personality	BF698
Developmental Psychology	BF712–724.85
Social Psychology	HM251–291
Educational Psychology	LB1051–1091
Physiological Psychology	QP351–499
Neuropsychology	QP360
Psychiatry	RC455
Clinical Psychology	RC467

2. Find where the dictionaries, encyclopaedias of Psychology, dictionaries of Psychology and other reference books are held in the library.
3. Test your understanding of the catalogue system some time before you need it. Do this by browsing for a title on the shelves and then use the catalogue to find that title.

4. Lecturers will put the excellent books you need on closed reserve. Often the books referred to on reading lists are held in a special section of the library where you may borrow them for short periods or photocopy them.

6.2.2 Bond and McConkey (2000)

Bond and McConkey (2000) is a general introduction to Psychology. You should always read this before venturing out to find more information for your essays and assignments. Note that no single section in Bond and McConkey (2000) will give a full outline of material related to your essay question or research assignment. Psychology is not neatly divided up into areas; textbooks are. Lecturers know this and will generally ask questions that require you to investigate a wide range of issues, covering many aspects of your textbook. You will need to examine the index to fully appreciate the connections between areas.

6.2.3 Reading books

The prime rule is that you must be an active reader. You cannot simply read a text and remember its contents. You must involve yourself in your reading but this does not mean taking out a highlighter or underlining the key terms. To assist your understanding of the text there are hundreds of multiple-choice questions on the Bond and McConkey Web page. Consider these as a better alternative to your highlighter, if for no other reason than that the multiple-choice questions will bear a close resemblance to your final examination. Comprehension comes with slow, deliberate reading. Better still, comprehension and maintenance of what you learn comes from a range of activities that you can employ.

■

> If in the last few years you haven't discarded a major opinion or acquired a new one, check your pulse. You may be dead.
> *Gelett Burgess*

THE SQ3R method

This method of reading for improving comprehension derives from Thomas and Robinson (1982), and Robinson (1970). The method outlined is good advice. There are five steps to reading for comprehension: survey, question, read, recite and review. Each step builds familiarity with the material and associations with what you are reading and what you need to remember for future reference.

Survey

Before you begin in earnest, skim the chapter. Look at the key terms and titles. Read the summary, read the learning objectives. This process has two benefits: you will not think the task is endless as you progress slowly through the chapter; you will gain an overview of the area you are assessing.

Look at the end of chapter questions. Read them all. You won't even know what they mean at this stage but as you read the chapter you will find the answers and each new answer will come as a discovery of sorts. You will remember those pieces of information.

Question

Ask yourself questions about the material. Guess which components might appear in an examination as multiple-choice questions and short answer questions. Ask yourself questions such as:

* What does this mean? What are the main points the author is trying to convey?
* What significance does this have for helping people, understanding the actions of people and so on?
* How could you test the idea? How did others test the idea?
* What did we once think about this idea?
* Does the material just reflect commonsense or would people who have not studied Psychology understand the point too?
* Does the material answer any of the end of chapter questions?

Read

Read the material and take notes of the definitions and key terms, outline the theories and write down the key research findings. Consider not using a highlighter in your book or even on the photocopied articles you obtain. The problem with highlighters is that they prevent you from absorbing the material because you will believe you have the point by outlining it in fluorescence. Some people end up highlighting most of an article! The better approach is to take rough notes and then convert these into review notes. When you can say the point in your own words and have asked questions about that idea and answered them, you have the point; you also have a set of review notes.

Recite

To recite is to keep asking yourself questions as you read. Find the answers to satisfy yourself that you know the point. Can you recall the main points? Can you explain the main points of the theory or can you describe in your own words how the research was performed? Check the text again to see if your recall is accurate.

Review

Your review should involve a test of whether you have covered all the material in the chapter. Start with the end of chapter summary. Did your reading get all the points in the summary? Next, look at the learning objectives. Can you say to yourself that you met those objectives? Finally, can you answer the end of chapter questions and those you raised?

You should now have a set of questions and answers to those questions. These will be your review notes. If you don't adopt the entire process outlined here, consider a cut-down version that involves a preview of the chapter, raising possible questions and reading to answer those questions. When you read the material, keep reminding yourself that your end of year examination will draw from this material. Can a question be formed from the material you just read? Can you answer that question?

■

> I never learned from a man who agreed with me.
>
> *Robert A. Heinlein*

6.2.4 Journal articles

Journal articles in Psychology are the products of original research. They are the laboratory reports, reviews, commentaries and theoretical arguments of scientists who work to advance Psychology as a discipline. When your lecturers research they generally aim to write up that research and present it to a journal for peer review. When other experts have examined their research and deemed it acceptable, it is printed in the journal. Journals are produced regularly, sometimes monthly, bimonthly or quarterly. Journal articles are generally complex and not often read by introductory students. However, you need to know what they are since your textbook, and almost everything you read about in Psychology, refers to these as the origins of information about Psychology.

The most recent journal articles are normally held in a special section of the library. You probably will not have borrowing rights on these and may not even have access to them. They are held on display for a period and no one has borrowing rights on them. You can look at these as a matter of interest but don't get too keen on reading them for your study. When a years' worth of journals have been in this section they a normally bound into volumes. Increasingly, journals are also being recorded electronically and stored on databases. When you write out your references, you record a volume number. The volume number is bolded in the example:

> Brown, J. D. (1986). Evaluations of self and others: Self-enhancement biases in social judgements. *Social Cognition*, *4*, 4, 353–76.

If you are asked to read a particular article, you will need to find where the journal is located in the library. Sometimes even the bound journals are held in special sections of the library, but normally they are held by title in the BF section along with the general texts. Your library's computer catalogue is the place to start. There are hundreds of different journals in Psychology so you should be aware that your library is unlikely to stock all of the journal titles. Find out whether the journal is subscribed to by checking the catalogue and then find where it is located. Once you find the journal section, you will easily find the volumes on the shelves. When you find the shelves of journals, you will be looking at the only thing you can actually point to that defines what is meant by the word 'psychology'. Run down the volume numbers until you hit the right one, look up the page reference.

As an exercise, look up the references in Bond and McConkey (2000). Find a journal article in that reference list that appears in any of the following:

- *American Psychologist*
- *The Australian Journal of Psychology*
- *The New Zealand Journal of Psychology*
- *Psychological Bulletin*
- *Journal of Experimental Psychology*
- *Journal of Social Psychology.*

These journals are likely to be held in your library. Find the article listed in Bond and McConkey (2000) in your library.

Finding the right journals to read

There are three main reasons why you might need to look up a journal article. You may find a reference to an article that deals with an issue that is something you need to research from:

- a textbook reference
- another journal's reference list
- a search you conduct on a computer database.

You may get copies of articles photocopied for you or placed on closed reserve. These may contain more references and you may want to obtain one or two of these. Don't get too serious with journal articles in your first year. It is possibly better to read collections of journal articles that are bound into edited books. These generally have titles such as *Readings in Social Psychology* or *Readings in the history of Psychology*. You will find one that interests you by browsing. These edited versions will have some introduction as to the significance of the contributions.

6.2.5 Psychlit

Psychlit is an electronic database of journal titles that can be searched using key terms, dates and author surnames. Researchers use Psychlit to examine a subject area and provide a list of all the books and journal articles written on a particular topic or all the publications of a particular author. Before computers a special journal called *Psychological Abstracts* listed the same sort of information. You will probably not use Psychlit, but even if you do have access to it, it isn't recommend until you have gained a thorough understanding of journals and referencing. You do need to know that lecturers, researchers and postgraduate students use computer catalogues when they start their research topics, although they will also look to a good text to put them on the right path.

6.2.6 Library computer catalogues

Libraries are fast becoming sophisticated at interfacing electronic databases to library users. This is in your best interests. Unlike the old card catalogue systems that are now rapidly disappearing from even quite small libraries, with computer catalogues you can rapidly access information of the collections of the library you are in, collections of other libraries you are not in, electronic catalogues of journal abstracts (e.g. Psychlit) and information on the World Wide Web. Most importantly, you can request books, reserve them, print copies of online journal articles and download information and files from the Internet. You can sometimes do this all from a single computer and some libraries are moving towards software that will simultaneously provide all these options for you within the context of a single search. Libraries will vary in their sophistication. Major university libraries normally have an Internet interface so that you can access the library at home. This is particularly useful for working outside of library hours and accessing references you may have forgotten, subject portals, online dictionaries, encyclopaedias and further advice on how to use the system.

A problem created by this revolution in technology that most people encounter when searching using an electronic resource is that of information overload. Typing in 'psychology' into any library database will give you thousands of titles. If you type 'Psychology' into the Web search engine LYCOS, you get 1 459 555 Internet sites about Psychology (this figure is constantly increasing). There are even 3885 sites that can be accessed when Psychology is spelt incorrectly as 'psycology' (the first to the home page of a Psychology department!). It is too much information and is not ordered in any particularly useful way. Some search engines recognise this and will immediately offer the instruction to refine your search with a link to help on how such things can be achieved.

Avoiding information overload

Here are some tips for dealing with search engines and information overload.

1. Be as specific as possible with your terms and place the most important ones first.
2. Learn to use the logical operators or expressions to refine your searching. Sometimes this is done with + and −, at other times 'Boolean' expressions of 'and', 'or', 'not', 'near'.

3. Brackets dramatically alter the meaning of your search. The expression 'Psychology and Philosophy' will give you all the matches for Psychology and all the matches for philosophy. Putting brackets around it so it appears (Psychology and Philosophy) will give you only those matches that contain both Psychology and philosophy.
4. Different search engine use different rules.
5. A library catalogue will normally give you specifications for searching on title, key words, author, subject key word, journal title and a range of others, including searching on the ISBN (a unique number assigned to every book).
6. Search engines are programmed to give you the most relevant titles first. If you do bring up a large list, only look at the first 20–30 items. Use these to give you an overview of how to refine your search.
7. Librarians have years of experience, specialised degrees in information searching and a magnificent grasp on the resources that are available to you. They are there to help you.
8. Finally, consider what you are trying to achieve with the electronic catalogue and consider not using it as the first entry point when gathering information for essays and assignments. It may be better first to browse the shelves, examine some books, certainly examine Bond and McConkey (2000), and gain an overview of the subject that you are examining. In this way, you will refine your understanding of the subject area, which will make your use of the databases far more efficient.

Encountering the technology

Your library will run training on the computer catalogue system: it is too sophisticated now for you to efficiently use the resource without some instruction. There will be information in the form of pamphlets that will assist you if you are reasonably familiar with some other similar system. You should learn how to access the databases from home if you have an Internet connection. If not, spend as much time as you can to learn about what is on offer with the computer catalogue at your library. You will find the investment of time useful as you progress past your first year.

■

If you think education is expensive, try ignorance!

Andy McIntyre

6.2.7 The World Wide Web

On the Bond and McConkey Web page there are links to sites organised in categories. Here you will find links to useful sites and resources. There are also chapter multiple-choice questions. For your researching purposes you need to be aware of one fact. Anyone can create a Web page. This is good because it allows a range of material to be introduced to a wide audience. However, not all the information is good information. You need to be careful when evaluating that material, and keep an open mind but a healthy level of scepticism.

Your first entry point to the Web and Psychology resources should be the Bond and McConkey Web page. Have a look at:
www.mcgraw-hill.com.au/mhhe/psychology/bond/

There are a series of links to resources on the Web. The list is by no means exhaustive but it should be useful. Many of the pages have their own lists of links, so you can explore more and more sites from this single entry point.

6.2.8 Reference material

Yearbooks

Yearbooks are produced by the government department for statistics. Yearbooks are useful for ensuring you have up-to-date statistics on what you are discussing in your essays. Yearbooks contain information on population demographics, road accidents, the number of people in different occupations, salaries, the number of people in different levels of education, the economy and so on. If you can include the latest statistics in your essay or assignment, then the small amount of effort it will take to gain this information will be rewarded. Yearbooks are held in most libraries in the reserve section or the reference only section.

Dictionaries of Psychology

You may like to get a copy of a dictionary of Psychology to help you with the terminology used in Psychology. You should be aware that the glossary of Bond and McConkey (2000) will generally cover most of the troublesome terms that you come across. Also, the Bond and McConkey Web page has links to online dictionaries.

Encyclopaedias of Psychology

Encyclopaedias of Psychology will be held in the reference section of your library. You should consult these regularly. Be aware that an encyclopaedia will be out of date almost before it appears on the shelf. You should limit your use of this resource to gain a general overview of a specific topic and consider the references that encyclopaedias refers to as primary and fundamental to the topic you are concerned with.

6.2.9 Help with grammar

There is a whole industry dedicated to helping you with your English. It will take some practice to acquire the sense of formal writing, learn how to be creative within its confines and know how to detect errors in your writing. Two things are certain: your computer spell checker will not pick up all the spelling errors but it will find most of them; a grammar checker will tell you that you a sentence is in the passive voice until you turn off that rule or avoid using the checker altogether. Reading about grammar does not improve your grammar; in the same sense, reading the dictionary will not improve your vocabulary. Getting your grammar right comes with practice.

Advice on resources for dealing with grammar

- Buy a dictionary—a thick hardcover one. Treasure it.
- Find a thin booklet that deals with grammar. Thick volumes are available but you will not be too sophisticated with your writing because formal writing confines the rules to basic issues of expression. Thick volumes become daunting when you are stuck on something because you have to wade through so much to find an answer. Thin booklets will get you to your answer quickly. If you cannot find the answer in your thin grammar guide, then rewrite the sentence for clarity. Keep it simple.
- The APA Manual offers some advice on writing and punctuation but it is expensive for you to buy. It is really designed for researchers and postgraduate students.

6.3 Lectures

Taking notes

Lecturers vary in the quality of their presentations and the supplementary material they will offer in the way of handouts, recommended readings and so on. Sometimes this variance is due to the subject they teach. Some subjects lend themselves to great lectures, others are harder to get through.

A few tips on getting through lectures and taking effective notes

You may take some time to settle in and warm to a lecture. Lecturers sometimes forget this and provide the most important material at the beginning of their lecture. In essays, texts and research reports, the definitions and fundamental concepts are explained at the beginning and built on in later discussion. Lectures are also organised this way. Be attentive at the outset! The fundamental concepts and the definitions are what will appear in the examination and these are outlined at the beginning of lectures. You may find the best notes are taken in the first 10 minutes.

It is often suggested that you should examine your notes immediately after class as your notes will need to be edited, organised and developed. These things are best done when the information is fresh in your mind. This is great advice but it does not reflect actual university study. First, you are likely to have another class immediately after your lecture. Further, lecturers vary in their skill of developing the material in one lecture. It may not be appropriate to review your notes until the second or third lecture in the particular series. In addition, the café will have that irresistible pull that develops over your time at university. Lectures can be exhausting work and a break is probably not a bad thing to consider. However, if you do not review your notes straight away, you are going have to consider them some time in the future so you need to take effective lecture notes for effective study.

> Great spirits have always faced violent protest from mediocre minds.
> *Albert Einstein*

The most mercenary way to take the best notes is to consider every lecture as a potential essay question in the mid year or end of year examination. In that examination you will be asked to write down 10 points about a particular area. Here are the points that develop from this view:

1. Write down anything the lecturer repeats.
2. Write down potential examination questions that you think the lecturer might ask.
3. Write down the areas that are covered as outlined on overheads or as a PowerPoint presentation.
4. Examine any handouts given to you. Don't repeat what a handout provides.
5. Pay careful attention to the research that is cited: why was the research conducted? what did they come up with?
6. Be aware that lecturers point to things that they do not develop in their lectures—develop an abbreviation to code what they point to. Later you will read about this in your textbook to fill out your notes.

When you review your notes, examine them for potential examination questions. If your notes can be developed into a good answer to an essay question, then start the process of researching the area by first examining Bond and McConkey (2000). Add to your notes and create a file for your essay questions. Examine the handouts. Ask yourself this question: 'If I had these notes in the end of year examination, could I answer a question worth 10 marks?'.

6.4 Frequently asked questions

Beyond my text what should I read?

You can read anything you are interested in reading. Browsing the shelves is the best way to get involved with a reading of Psychology. You should do this as often as you can, recognising that you have so much to read anyway. It is doubtful that a first year Psychology student (or anyone for that matter) couldn't become absorbed by a topic in Psychology. To become absorbed you will need to graze the books. Skim through a few, put down those that seem tedious or too technical, find those that you enjoy reading. This activity is not wasteful. You will find yourself including this material in examinations and essays at some later time.

Should I read and take notes for a chapter at a time?

Maybe. In Bond and McConkey (2000, Chapter 8) you will discover that *spaced* learning is superior to *massed* learning. The trick is to read and review your text regularly. Whether you can read a chapter at a time isn't as important as taking in the information. Your ability to work efficiently for longer periods of time (and therefore a chapter at a time) will develop. When you are reviewing, ask yourself whether you are being effective; test yourself. You may find yourself starting out in 20-minute blocks, then 30 minutes, then hour long periods.

But I like using a highlighter and you imply this is wrong?

Highlight no more than 10–15% of the material you are reading.

I have a really poor memory. Help?

Having a poor memory isn't the difficulty. You will find a lot of suggestions to improve your memory in Chapter 10 of Bond of McConkey (2000). Learning Psychology is about knowing how psychologists go about tasks. Some of those tasks are more practical tasks, such as carrying out research, and some of them are conceptual tasks, such as designing experiments. Knowing a text is not about remembering it, it's about remembering how psychologists approach topics. You are not learning facts; you are learning how to go about things.

How could I possibly get a complete list of the material for the essay topic and read it all to produce the essay? I'd have to read for months!

Actually, you would probably have to read for decades! Often postgraduate students get tangled with this issue as they produce theses. The problem isn't one of time. It's a truism that you cannot read all there is to know about any topic—you couldn't possibly read all the books in the library. By the time you finished reading even a shelf or two there would be a whole new set of information to read. You would be like the painters of the Sydney Harbour Bridge—perpetually painting the Bridge because by the time they finish it needs repainting.

Perhaps you are not so desperate to read everything but you want to convince yourself you have not missed something crucial. In either case, the concern is misplaced. Ask yourself whether, if you wanted to know an aspect of mathematics, say addition, you would need to complete every conceivable addition. No. You would only read a few books to grasp the rule and provide sufficient exposure to examples to ensure you can apply it. The same is true of essay material. Learn the argument; illustrate it with a few examples. You don't need to read every example to be able to convey your point. You need sufficient evidence, not every piece of evidence.

Remember, rely on your text. People who have read books and journals in Psychology for decades have produced your textbook. The textbook provides you with a good guide through the mass of material you could encounter. That's what textbooks are for.

CHAPTER 7
DEALING WITH STATISTICS

OVERVIEW

Reducing fears about things statistical
7.1   Step 1 Starting out with statistics
7.2   Step 2 First statistics: mean, median, mode
7.3   Step 3 Analysing variability: z-scores
7.4   Step 4 Types of variables
7.5   Step 5 The Pearson product moment correlation coefficient
7.6   Step 6 The t-test
7.7   Approaching statistics examinations
7.8   Frequently asked questions
7.9   Answers to exercises

REDUCING FEARS ABOUT THINGS STATISTICAL

Almost everyone studying Psychology has an aversion to the statistical side of psychological inquiry. It is hoped that in this chapter any fear of statistics, for example, when you see the formula for the t-test, will be reduced. Statistics is a matter of practice within Psychology. Thus, exercises and questions for you to work through are presented here. As you progress through these exercises, it is hoped you will develop a practical understanding of statistics to a point where you have some confidence with those tests outlined in the text.

∎

The conventional view serves to protect us from the painful job of thinking.
                                                              J. K. Galbraith

Chapter 2 of Bond and McConkey (2000) tells you what statistics are and how they are used in Psychology. Chapter 4 of this Guide tells you how to present them in your reports. You will need to read all the relevant text in Bond and McConkey (2000) before you begin here. It will also help you to have it alongside as you progress through the problems. Instructions about the rules for presenting graphs and figures can be found on pages 65–68.

This is not a complete guide to statistics. The aim is to start with relatively simple mathematics, such as adding fractions, and progress in steps until it is possible to compute the Pearson product moment correlation coefficient and the student's t-test. Large areas of statistics will be missed on this journey. However, it is hoped that you will develop confidence with statistics so that when you confront statistics in your course you will not be put off by what seems complex and sophisticated. This chapter should be read as a guide to reducing statistical anxiety, with helpful hints to complement your instruction elsewhere. Finally, as with the other chapters there are some frequently asked questions for which some answers are provided.

Statistics in Psychology has little to do with mathematics!

You may not really understand the physical hardware of the Internet, TCP/IP protocols and hardware handshaking, yet you probably can navigate around the Internet well enough, find useful information and have fun with it. Not many people get too engrossed with understanding fibre optic cables when they make a telephone call, yet no one doubts the benefit of telephone calls. So, too, with statistics.

Statisticians understand the very technical mathematics that underpins statistical techniques. However, part of a statistician's job is to research and promote statistical methods for other researchers to use. In doing this, statisticians deal with the mathematics, not the logic of the employment of statistics. Statisticians create methods, they are not so concerned how they are used. In fact, before computers became common, statisticians developed a number of statistical techniques that were mathematically feasible but practically impossible to use. The complexity of some procedures involved a log–linear analysis, which would mean just one analysis would take months of calculations!

However, when psychologists use statistics they primarily employ logical operations, not mathematical ones (Babbie, 1995); they leave the mathematics aside for statisticians to deal with. Similarly, when you make a telephone call to your grandmother, you perform a social operation not a technical one; you leave the technicalities of fibre optics to engineers.

As a researcher it is important to present information about one's reasoning about the topic of investigation. Statistical procedures provide a set of ready-made logical operations that bring about reasonable conclusions, provided the statistics are applied appropriately. It is like ensuring the telephone is in good order and dialling the right number. Statistics are, in themselves, sets of shortcuts of reasoning; they provide a convenient way to present a set of reasoning about information. Statistical operations within Psychology are as different from mathematics as telephone calls are to cellular networks. You need not fear that with ever-increasing levels of statistics it is going to get tougher and tougher for you mathematically. You will need some basic understanding of mathematics but beyond that it's all about application, that is, knowing how to use statistics.

Only a certain type of person is good at statistics!

The idea that only some people are good at statistics is not true when considering the employment of statistical techniques in Psychology. Even if you have some stereotype it does not necessarily hold when we start talking about using statistical techniques. You can be good at statistics without some special sort of genetic endowment. In fact, if you can follow a set of instructions, just like baking a cake, you too can succeed in developing a great understanding of the employment of statistics.

■

Since when was genius found respectable?
Elizabeth Barrett Browning

7.1 Step 1 Starting out with statistics

You will need some basic mathematics to be able to employ statistics. Thus, some revision of high school mathematics is provided below as a prompt in case it is material you have forgotten.

Equations

Try the following exercises (the answers can be found on p. 136). Don't worry if you struggle, just move through to the explanation section that follows. These explanations should prompt you to remember.

Pre-testing: Exercise set 7.1

Solve the following.

1. $\dfrac{4}{8} + \dfrac{7}{12} = x$

2. $\dfrac{3}{4} \times \dfrac{7}{8} = x$

3. $\dfrac{12}{5} \div \dfrac{3}{5} = x$

4. $\sqrt{169} = x$ 5. $\dfrac{x^2}{25} = 1$ 6. $25^4 + \sqrt{225} = x$

Explanations

1 Adding fractions

You can do this on your calculator—you just divide 4 by 8 and get 0.5. Then you divide 7 by 12 and you get 0.583 33. If you add these, you get 1.083 33. This is fine for simple operations but you might get tangled with understanding more complex formulae that you encounter. What you need to understand is the operation. Here it is in full:

$$\frac{4}{8} + \frac{7}{12} = \frac{(4 \times 12) + (7 \times 8)}{8 \times 12} = \frac{104}{96}$$

Remember that the final numerator (the top part of the fraction) is the sum of the two numerators multiplied by the other fraction's denominator (the bottom part of the fraction). The final denominator is the product of the two denominators.

2 Multiplying fractions

It is easy to multiply fractions. The final numerator is the product of the two numerators and the final denominator is the product of the two denominators.

$$\frac{3}{4} \times \frac{7}{8} = \frac{(3 \times 7)}{(4 \times 8)} = \frac{21}{32} = 0.66$$

3 Dividing fractions

To divide fractions, simply multiply the fraction that is the numerator (top) by the reciprocal of the fraction that represents the denominator (bottom). That is, you take the second fraction's numerator (top) and invert it so it's the denominator (bottom), and invert its denominator (bottom) so that it's the numerator (top).

$$\frac{12}{5} \div \frac{3}{5} = \frac{12}{5} \times \frac{5}{3} = \frac{(12 \times 5)}{(5 \times 3)} = \frac{60}{15} = \frac{4}{1} = 1$$

4 The square root

Be aware that the square root function is an important one; it is easiest to perform on your calculator. You should also note that the reciprocal function (the opposite and, therefore, related function) is the base quantity raised to the power of 2 or x^2 (meaning $x \times x$ or the value of x multiplied by itself). It will often appear as x^2 or $x{\wedge}2$ on your calculator, and you can apply the inverse function to obtain the square root of a value. The $x{\wedge}2$ is invariably used for computers and within spreadsheet packages such as Excel.

$$\sqrt{169} = x$$
$$13 \times 13 = 169$$
$$x = 13$$

5 Solving equations

Remember, whatever you do to one side, you do to the other:

$$\frac{x^2}{25} = 1$$
$$x^2 = 25$$
$$x = \sqrt{25}$$
$$x = 5$$

6 Raised powers

You know from question 5 that $x^2 = x \times x$; now you have $x \times x \times x \times x$ (where $x = 25$). Again, you should use a calculator. The function you need will look like x^y or $x{\wedge}y$. From there the equation is simple to solve.

$$25 \times 25 \times 25 \times 25 + \sqrt{225} = x$$
$$390\,625 + 15 = x$$
$$x = 390\,640$$

■

> I've never let my school interfere with my education.
>
> *Mark Twain*

Post-testing: Exercise set 7.2

Solve the following. (*Note*: Remember to do what is in brackets first.)

1. $\dfrac{12}{17} + \left(\dfrac{14}{19} \times \dfrac{2}{3}\right)$
   2. $\dfrac{7}{5} + \left(\dfrac{4^2}{13} \div \dfrac{12}{5}\right)$
   3. $5^3 \times \sqrt{25}$

4. $\dfrac{23}{5^2} \times \sqrt{64}$ 5. 6^4 6. $\dfrac{\left(12+13+15+16+18\right)}{5}$

What you should know

- Adding, multiplying and dividing fractions.
- Squared and square root functions.
- Operations on equations.
- Calculating raised powers.

7.2 Step 2 First statistics: mean, median, mode

The first statistics you will encounter are normally the mean, median and mode. The mean, in particular, is a very common statistic. If you have done question 6 in Exercise 7.2 you have already performed the operation of calculating the mean. Calculating the mean is simply adding up the values in your set of data and dividing by how many values you have added up. An explanation of the mean and its function is given on page P1.42 of Bond and McConkey (2000). Here it is again, in full:

$$\overline{X} = \frac{\sum_{i=1}^{N} \overline{X}_i}{N}$$

What does this mean? The $\overline{X}$ means the average of the sample X (the set X, made up of individual units, i). The bar above the X indicates that the result of the equation is the mean—anything with a bar on top is the mean. The rest of the equation is a simple fraction, like those you have done above. The Σ (Greek upper case sigma) means to 'add together the following ...' or, in more technical language, it indicates to 'take the sum of ...' or just 'the sum of ...'. The little i is the place you start, here defined by the 1 as the first value in your set of X (your data) . The N at the top of sigma is where you finish; it is the last number in the set of X. Thus, you have a start and a finish, and an operation—'add them up'. That is, add all the values in set X together, starting at the first one and finishing with the last one. N is the number of elements of the set X or your sample size. Thus, you add the numbers together and divide by how many you have. You end up with $\overline{X}$, the mean.

Pre-testing: Describing data: Exercise set 7.3

1. Calculate the mean, median and mode of the following sample of vehicle speeds:

68.1 49.8 56.7 55.6 55.4 55.4 60.8 72.5 42.3
50.6 54.5 55.2 58.6 62.3 45.2 52.4 40.5 52.3

2. Is the data skewed?
3. If you were to pick the fifth number in the first row of the sample above (i.e. 55.4) would you have created a statistic?
4. If the data in question 1 is defines as the set Z, then solve the following:

$$\sum_{i=1}^{4} Z_i =$$

5. Again, using the data in question 1, solve the following:

$$\left(\sum_{i=3}^{7} z_i \right)^2 =$$

Answers and explanation

1. Mean = 54.9, median = 55.3; mode = 55.4.

   Remember the trick with calculating the median is to order the data from lowest to highest and select the middle number. When there are an even number of data, add the middle two together and divide by 2.

2. Yes: the mean is less than the median and the median is less then the mode.

   Here is a trick to aid your memory. 'Mean', 'median' and 'mode' can be ordered alphabetically. When the order is mean, median, mode (i.e. their alphabetical order), the skew is negative. If the order is reversed (i.e. mode, median, mean), then the data are positively skewed.
   When you are shown graphs of distributions (Fig. 2.11, Bond & McConkey, 2000), you will need to remember that a negative skew occurs when the tail points to the left and a positive skew occurs if it points to the right.

3. Yes. A statistic is simply a function on samples, such that any sample is paired with a value of that statistic. (Hays, 1988). In fact, you could dream up the number 60 to represent your sample and that would be a statistic, although perhaps not a very useful one. Put very simply, a statistic is a number used to represent a set of data. Its 'language' equivalent is a title; it is simply something that is paired with the data you are trying to represent, just as a title describes information in the text. Titles are meant to be useful in that they should accurately reflect the text; we use techniques to make our statistics useful.

4. 230.2

   The formula states, 'Sum the values i in set Z starting at value 1 and finishing at value 4'. You add up the first four values to get 230.2.

5. 80 599.21

This time the formula states, 'Sum the values i in set Z, starting at value 3 and finishing at value 7', then square the value (you are going to use this formula again below).

Post-testing: Exercise set 7.4

1. Calculate the mean, median and mode for the following data that estimates distance in centimetres. Define the set of data as Z for the questions that follow.

> 11.2   16.5   14.2   14.1   16.6   14.5   15.3   15.3   15.4
>
> 12.9   13.8   15.4   11.2   14.6   15.4   14.8   15.6   14.3

2. In which direction is the data skewed?

3. $\displaystyle\sum_{i=1}^{4} Z_i =$

4. $\displaystyle\sum_{i=4}^{8} Z_i =$

5. Calculate the following:

$$\sum_{i=4}^{8} (Z_i)^2 =$$

(*Hint*: Do it in steps. Start inside the brackets.)

What you should know

- How to calculate the mean, median and mode.
- How to decide whether a sample has a skewed distribution.
- That statistics are not necessarily meaningful or complex.

7.3 Step 3 Analysing variability: z-scores

This next step requires that you understand those statistics that describe variability. Bond and McConkey (2000) describes in detail the three you need to know: the variance, standard deviation (*SD*), and the sum of squares (*SS*). Table 2.2 describes the calculation for each of these, relying on first obtaining the sum of squares and deriving the other statistics from this statistic. In this section you will go one step further and calculate z-scores. However, before doing so an important issue must first be addressed or else all the calculations you perform below may go astray.

The difference between a sample and a population

The sample variance and the sample standard deviation have been used in all the calculations below, which is what you will need to use as well or your answers will be slightly different from those provided. The population variance and the population *SD* are presented in Bond and McConkey (2000, Chapter 2).

If you use a calculator to help you with your calculations, then you will have two choices for the calculation of the variance and, likewise, two choices for the calculation of the *SD*. The same is true if you use a software package like Excel to do your calculations. The difference between these often confuses students trying to calculate statistics in Psychology, especially because your are asked to make these calculations relying on steps and a calculator and you might be aware of the statistical functions that can be used as a shortcut or a way to verify what you have done. Still, because you get two choices for the *SD*, for example, your attempt to use a calculator's functionality to verify what you have done is no good. You need to know which of the choices to use.

What is the difference? In Bond and McConkey (2000) the *SS* is divided by *N* to get the variance. This is the population variance. If you take the square root of this, you will get the *SD*, but this is the population *SD*. If, instead, you divide the *SS* by *N* – 1, you will get the sample variance. If you take the square root of this, you will get the sample *SD*. On a calculator, the population *SD*, like that used in Bond and McConkey (2000), will almost always appear as the symbol σ (Greek lower case sigma). The sample *SD* normally appears as 'SD' or perhaps even σ – 1. In Excel, the statistical functions will help you out by providing an explanation of the difference: the population variance is VARP and the sample variance is VAR. The population *SD* is STDEVP and the STDEV is used for the sample *SD*.

Psychologists normally collect information about a sample to determine characteristics of a population. Thus, a sample, especially a random sample of, say, students' attitudes, is supposed to represent the population of students (let's say the population is the students at the university). When we obtain a statistic, we are generally talking about something that describes a sample (just those we have selected at random and surveyed). If we surveyed all the students at the university, we could then describe the variability of their attitudes towards smoking, for example, and we would use the population variance to get that estimate of the variance in attitudes. (We sometimes call this estimate of variability a parameter estimate, rather than a statistic—don't worry about the terminology difference, in practice it is the same sort of thing.) If we randomly selected 100 students from the population of thousands, then we would normally use the sample variance to estimate the attitudes of students. As the sample size increases (e.g. from 10 to 300), the difference between the population estimate and the sample estimate (i.e. whether you use σ or σ – 1) is minute. (If you think about it, dividing the SS by 9 instead of 10 will have a much greater impact than dividing the SS by 299 instead of 300.) You will have an intuitive feel for the fact that surveying 10 people for their attitudes is likely to be a far less accurate representation of the attitudes of the whole student population than a survey of 300 people. This is the reason for the adjustment to the sample variance. Taking 1 off the total sample corrects for that likelihood of being inaccurate and the impact of this decreases as the sample size gets closer and closer to the population size.

The important points are that psychologists distinguish between samples and populations. You have a choice on you calculator but for the following sections you should use the sample variance and the sample SD. This will mean that instead of N you will use N – 1 and, if you are using a calculator's statistical functions, you need SD (sometimes it's represented as σ – 1) and not σ. The reason is that the examples are practical and we are talking about samples, not populations.

Pre-testing: *SS*, variance and *SD*: Exercise set 7.5

Before calculating z-scores it is best to determine that you can calculate the variance and standard deviation by following the outline described in Table 2.2 of Bond and McConkey (2000). Use the steps provided there to answer the following.

1. Sixteen pilots were assessed on a test determining their knowledge of navigation. The maximum score for the test was 200. Calculate the sum of squares, variance and standard deviation for these scores.

   | 130 | 134 | 122 | 122 | 156 | 145 | 167 | 90 |
   | 89 | 142 | 163 | 152 | 146 | 121 | 129 | 170 |

2. Now, transform the data into percentages. Are the sum of squares, variance and standard deviation different from your answers in question 1?

Explanation

A z-score is a transformation of data. You made a transformation when you changed the data into percentages in Exercise set 7.5. In other words, you altered your data mathematically so that the same data appear differently. The transformation involved in a z-score is a process sometimes called 'standardisation'. Each datum is transformed into what is known as a standard score, which in this case means that each piece of data is transformed into standard deviation units. Standard deviation units are explained in Bond and McConkey (2000, p. P1.43).

You know that for a normal distribution, a bell curve, a certain percentage of the population will fall between 1 standard deviation from the mean. In fact, 68.27% fall within 1 standard deviation.

For example, a normal curve describing IQ scores with a mean of 100 and an *SD* of 13 will indicate that most people (68.27% of people) have an IQ score between 87 and 113. It becomes less likely that anyone you sample would have an IQ score higher or lower than this the more extreme his or her scores become. Thus, it is rare to find people with an IQ score of 139, and rare to find people with an IQ score of 50. z-scores help to show how rare things are in a population by indicating how far each item is from the mean, through transformation of data, such as a percentage, into standard deviation units.

z-scores are calculated by the following formula:

$$z_i = \frac{X_i - \overline{X}}{S_X}$$

The steps are straightforward:

- For any value *i* from sample *X*, subtract the mean of the sample *X* and then divide by the standard deviation of *X*. First you must calculate the mean and standard deviation of the sample, which you know how to do from the above.

Suppose you want to calculate *z* for your driving speed on the motorway. You are driving at 115 kph and you know the average speed is 104.3 kph with a standard deviation of 6.3 kph.

$$z_i = \frac{115_i - 104.3}{6.3} = \frac{10.7}{6.3} = +1.6984$$

This z-score can then be used to determine how common it is for people to be found driving at such a speed. By examining a statistical table[14] of z-scores and their relation to a normal distribution, it is possible to determine how far away from the mean your individual score is, just as it is possible to say how rare an IQ score is in relation to a known mean and standard deviation. Given this example, only 4.55% of people would drive faster than you under these conditions; alternatively, when driving at 115 kph, you are driving faster than 95.46% of the population.

---

[14] It is possible to calculate the same figure but it isn't necessary to consider it here. You will need to find a statistical table for the purpose, which most introductory statistics books have. You can use a spreadsheet package such as Excel to obtain the figure by using the NORMDIST function. You have to convert the figure it returns by subtracting it from 1 and then multiplying by 100.

Post-testing: Exercise set 7.6

Suppose you want to know which area of study you are particularly good at compared with others you know who have different talents. You look at your grading on the following activities:

	Your score	Mean	SD	z
Reasoning	79	66	14.2	
Writing	75	50	16.8	
Statistics	66	53	4.7	

1. Calculate the z-score for each of the skills.
2. Which test score is the best relative to others?
3. Using the data from Exercise 7.5, take the first value (130) and calculate a z-score. Using the values for your transformed data (i.e. the mean and SD of the percentages), calculate the z-score for the same first value (it should be 65%). Are the z-scores that you calculate different?

What you should know

- How to calculate the SS, variance and SD.
- The difference between a population and a sample.
- How to calculate z-scores.

7.4 Step 4 Types of variables

Pre-testing: Exercise set 7.7

Describe the independent (IV) and dependent (DV) variables in the following studies:

1. A researcher measures the difference in weight gain in rats who are reared in a dimly lit condition and those reared in a brightened environment.
2. A sample of 1000 people are asked to decide between three political candidates.
3. The reaction times of drivers of various ages are assessed.
4. A researcher compares the rank preference of preschool and school-aged children to five different types of cereal brands.
5. A clinician compares the frequency of depression in prisoners and the normal population.

6. A researcher records the recognition of items from a list and compares the frequency of correct recall to the order in which the items are presented.

Answers and explanation

Students often get entangled with the idea of an independent variable. It is practical to remember a shortcut, although it doesn't exactly explain the concept. Make sure you understand the material in Bond and McConkey (2000, p. P1.28) that outlines the concept. However, for practical purposes the independent variable is the 'thing' that is manipulated by the researcher. If the researcher can alter it, then it is likely to be the independent variable. In question 2 above, the political candidate cannot be changed by the researcher in that the researcher does not alter the electoral process, but whether the researcher includes a particular candidate in their survey is under the researcher's direct control. Thus, it is the three choices given to the participants that is the independent variable— what choice the researcher offers is under the researcher's control.

The dependent variable is entirely out of the researcher's control. There cannot be altered. The dependent variable is not to be altered, rather measured. The dependent variable is always the 'thing' measured by the researcher.

- Independent variable: 'thing' manipulated; 'thing' within the researcher's control.
- Dependent variable: 'thing' measured.

■

> The world is a tragedy to those who feel, but a comedy to those who think.   *Horace Walpole*

Post-testing: Variables: Exercise set 7.8

1. For each of the independent and dependent variables in question 2, outline what sort of variable is being manipulated or recorded. If you are up to some extension, think about what sort of statistical test might be employed for questions 1 and 3.

What you should know

- Know the difference between different types of variables.
- Know how to recognise which is the independent variable and which is the dependent variable.

- Understand that the type of variables determines the types of statistical test available to the researcher.

7.5 Step 5 The Pearson product moment correlation coefficient

The Pearson product moment correlation coefficient is a versatile way to calculate the correlation between two variables. There are other methods for calculating the correlation between two variables (e.g. the Spearman rank order correlation) and in the past there have been shortcuts for calculating the correlation when one variable has only two values (the point–biserial correlation). Nowadays, with computers to do the calculations, the Pearson product moment correlation coefficient is the most commonly used method. Computer programs will almost always use the Pearson product moment correlation coefficient to do the calculations even though the statistical package might give you the option for a test with another name. The Spearman rank order correlation, for example, is mathematically equivalent to the Pearson product moment correlation coefficient but has more limitations on its use so is not widely used.

Here is a computational formula for the Pearson product moment correlation coefficient:

$$r_{xy} = \frac{\sum_{i=1}^{N} zx_i zy_i}{N-1}$$

This formula looks complex but you already have a few hints as to what the notation stands for. In fact, this is a condensed version of the computational formula but since you already know how to calculate z-scores we will use this one. Let's unpack the notation. The r is a symbol to indicate 'correlation'. Here it is between the two variables we can call X and Y denoted by the subscripts. It could be between any two variables, so something such as $r_{big, small}$ is reasonably acceptable. However, when defining the formula, algebraic units are used, so we use X and Y as placeholders for our variables. The denominator is easy enough. It is the total number of data points minus 1. The top line has two z-scores.

Steps for the calculation

The formula is easy to work through. There are four steps to follow:

1. Transform each variable into a set of z-scores.
2. Multiply the first z-score of set X by the first z-score in set Y.
3. Sum the product of the set of paired z-scores together.
4. Divide by the number of pairs minus 1.

Example

Driver	Engine size (cc rating) (X)	Speed (kph) (Y)
1	1500	55.6
2	1800	57.8
3	1000	50.5
4	2000	60.2
5	1600	58.5
6	2400	62.3
7	1600	52.5

Step 1

Transform both sets X and Y to z-scores:

$\overline{X} = 1700, \ SD_X = 439.89$
$\overline{Y} = 56.77, \ SD_Y = 4.19$

Driver	Engine size (cc rating) (X)	Speed (kph) (Y)
1	−0.4588	−0.2796
2	0.2294	0.2455
3	−1.6059	−1.4969
4	0.6882	0.8184
5	−0.2294	0.4126
6	1.6059	1.3196
7	−0.2294	−1.0195

Step 2

Multiply the z-scores together.

Driver	Engine size (cc rating) (X)	Speed (kph) (Y)	$z_X z_Y$
1	−0.4588	−0.2796	0.1283
2	0.2294	0.2455	0.0563
3	−1.6059	−1.4969	2.4039
4	0.6882	0.8184	0.5632
5	−0.2294	0.4126	−0.0947
6	1.6059	1.3196	2.1192
7	−0.2294	−1.0195	0.2339
Total			5.4102

Step 3

Sum the product of the z-scores. That is, add up the scores in the column you created in step 2.

$$5.4102 = 0.1283 + 0.0563 + 2.4039 + 0.5632 + (-0.0947) + 2.1192 + 0.2339$$

Step 4

Calculate the correlation by dividing the answer in step 3 by $N - 1$ (i.e. 6 as there are 7 drivers minus 1).

$$r_{xy} = \frac{\sum_{i=1}^{N} zx_i zy_i}{N - 1} = \frac{5.4102}{6} = +0.9017$$

It is important to indicate the direction of the correlation since a correlation coefficient can range from −1.00 to +1.00. You need to be able to interpret the result. Here the correlation between engine size and vehicle speed is very highly positively correlated, indicating that as engine size increases so does the vehicle speed.

Post-testing: Exercise set 7.9

1. Calculate the correlation coefficient for the following sets of data, interpret the results and provide a written description of the finding.

Student	Sensation seeking	Popularity
1	10	78
2	8	68
3	5	42
4	7	53
5	8	75
6	7	68
7	12	57
8	15	48
9	4	52
10	14	89

What you should know

- How to calculate the Pearson product moment correlation coefficient.
- That the Pearson product moment correlation coefficient replaces all other calculations of correlation.
- Be more familiar with the application of z-scores.

7.6 Step 6 The *t*-test

The steps for the calculation for the independent samples *t*-test are outlined in Bond and McConkey (2000), along with an example (pp. P1.51–P1.54). What you need to know here is that there are different types of *t*-tests: the repeated measures, or dependent samples, *t*-test, and the independent samples *t*-test. There is also a one-group *t*-test, although this will not be considered here.

The dependent measures *t*-test is used when each member of the first sample you are interested in has some association to a member of the second group you are interested in. Most commonly this arises when the member of the first group is the same person in the second group: this person provides two pieces of information that you assess. The dependent samples *t*-test is often referred to as a repeated measures *t*-test or a within-subjects *t*-test in circumstances in which the same participant provides two pieces of information. Technically, the participants experience all values of the independent variable. For example, suppose you are interested in the effectiveness of a particular drug for controlling attention deficit hyperactivity disorder (ADHD). Suppose you measure the concentration span of children with ADHD before the drug, then you measure the concentration span in the same children once they are placed on the drug regimen. The independent variable is the 'before/after' or 'without the drug/with the drug' measure. Since all participants experience both levels of the independent variable, you must use the dependent variable *t*-test to determine whether the group of children increases or decreases its concentration span with the drug.

Pre-testing: *t*-tests: Exercise set 7.10

For the following, determine whether the appropriate test is a dependent sample *t*-test or an independent sample *t*-test.

1. A researcher wishes to examine the difference between reading ability for a group of 12-year-old children and 14-year-old children.
2. A neurophysiologist examines the effect of a drug by comparing the improvement in activity in rats given the drug to those of a control group of rats not given the drug.
3. Professor Blithe examines his class' scores on a comprehension test of Psychology before and after his lectures.

4. A researcher records the attitudes of groups of people towards politicians before and after an election.
5. A human resource adviser examines the success of two different testing techniques for placing people in management positions.

Dependent samples *t*-test

The computational formula for the dependent samples *t*-test is:

$$t = \frac{\overline{D}}{\sqrt{\dfrac{\sum D^2 - \left[\left(\sum D\right)^2 / n\right]}{n(n-1)}}}$$

D stands for the difference between each pair of numbers in the samples you collected. The degrees of freedom (*df*) is calculated on the pairs, not the individual groups of numbers, and so it is the number of pairs minus 1 (*df* = *n* − 1). Be aware that the *df* for the independent samples is $(n_1 - 1) + (n_2 - 1)$ or the total number of observations minus 2.

This formula looks fairly complicated. However, if you have worked through the examples above you will have reached the point now where this formula can be easily read, and you know that reading it is about breaking it up into steps. You have already achieved all you need to know to be able to encounter this new formula.

Let's start at the top of the formula. Any symbol with a bar across the top of it represents a mean. As *D* represents the differences between the samples, $\overline{D}$ represents the mean of the differences between the samples.

This is step 1 in the calculation. You simply need to subtract the second score from the first score and you get a difference, *D*. Add together all the differences in the pairs and you get the total difference. Divide this by the number of pairs and you get the mean difference or $\overline{D}$.

The square root sign goes over the whole of the denominator, so we leave this to last. The two sigma signs operate like those encountered for calculating the sum of the squares for the correlation coefficient. That is, you have to total the squared differences in the first instance and obtain the total of the differences squared in the second instance. Different statistical techniques operate with the same underlying logic so that the operations within them are similar across different sorts of tests. In fact, the *t*-test and the correlation coefficient formula are related tests: it is possible to convert one into another—although we will not consider it here.

Steps for the calculation

1. Determine the difference between the scores and total these differences, ΣD.
2. Divide the sum of the differences by the number of scores to find the mean difference, $\overline{D}$.
3. Square the difference in scores and total these to find the sum of the square differences, ΣD^2.
4. Square the sum of the differences (i.e. the value in step 1) and divide by n.
5. Subtract the result of step 4 from the result in step 3 and divide by $n(n-1)$.
6. Take the square root of step 5.
7. Divide the result of step 2 by the result in step 6.
8. Interpret the results.

Example of a dependent samples *t*-test

The first three steps can be shown within one table. You should draw up a similar table to illustrate your working when calculating *t*.

Steps 1–3

	Student	Before	After	Step 1 D	Step 3 D^2
	1	20	21	1	1
	2	25	28	3	9
	3	24	24	0	0
	4	21	30	9	81
	5	19	25	6	36
	6	19	24	5	25
	7	23	26	3	9
	8	26	24	-2	4
	9	16	22	6	36
	10	18	17	-1	1
Step 2	Mean			3	
Step 1	Total			30	202

Step 1: $\Sigma D = 30$
Step 2: $\overline{D} = 3$
Step 3: $\Sigma D^2 = 202$

Step 4: Square the sum of the differences (i.e. the value in step 1) and divide by n.

$$\frac{\sum(D^2)}{n} = \frac{30^2}{10} = \frac{900}{10} = 90$$

Step 5: Subtract the result of step 4 from the result in step 3 and divide by $n(n-1)$.

$$\frac{202 - 90}{10(10-1)} = \frac{112}{(10 \times 9)} = \frac{112}{90} = 1.2444$$

Step 6: Take the square root of step 5.

$$\sqrt{1.2444} = 1.1155$$

Step 7: Divide the result of step 2 by the result in step 6.

$$t_{\overline{D}} = \frac{3}{1.1155} = +2.6894t$$

Step 8: Interpret the results (see Bond & McConkey, 2000, Chapter 2).

Post-testing: t-test: Exercise set 7.11

For the following sets of data, decide which type of t-test is appropriate, calculate t and write a written description of your finding.

1. Sally recorded the time 6-day-old infants took to scan two different facial images.

Infant	Image 1	Image 2
1	30.2	20.5
2	36.5	14.8
3	40.2	16.5
4	15.8	17.8
5	19.5	19.4
6	18.4	25.3
7	25.6	20.5
8	18.9	12.2

2. Professor Blithe examined the times two groups of rats spent in a maze locating a food pellet.

	Group 1 (X)	Group 2 (Y)
1	56	25
2	58	26
3	54	24
4	53	31
5	57	34
6	51	26
7	56	29
8	54	34
9	45	32
10	48	44

3. A university records officer tracks eight students through matriculation for their first year and their second year. The officer records the times and wishes to analyse the results.

Student	Hours in matriculation	
	First year	Second year
1	1.5	0.5
2	6	0.6
3	5	0.8
4	4	0.9
5	2.3	3
6	2.5	2
7	2.9	1.2
8	5	4

What you should know

- Know the difference between the dependent and independent samples *t*-tests.
- Know how to calculate the dependent samples *t*-test.
- Know how to calculate the independent samples *t*-test.

7.7 Approaching statistics examinations

Below is an outline of topics frequently covered in first year statistics for Psychology and, thus, an outline of those things you might need to know when you start revising for your examination. Past examinations are the key to success—you need to go over as many as you can. Also, see Chapter 8 of this Guide for general advice on dealing with Psychology examinations. Most of what applies to other examinations will apply to your statistics examination.

There is one special piece of advice for statistical examinations: show your working! Even if you don't get the right answer you will score marks for your working. The right answer by itself may not even gain the best grade because often lecturers will have a marking schedule that awards points for each step in the calculation. If you just put down the answer, even if it is correct, you may not get awarded the full marks for the question. Lecturers want to know that you know how to use statistics, and the only real way to determine this is for you to demonstrate the reasoning process you have employed. Remember, it is all about employing statistical tests logically, not mathematically, so if you get the right answer you have only done half the job because you should always write a written description of what the result means.

An outline of a statistics examination

1 Understanding statistical concepts

- Population
- Sample
- Inferential statistics
- Significance
- Positive and negative relationships
- Independent and dependent variables
- Variable types: nominal/dichotomous, ordinal, interval, ratio

2 Describing data

- Calculating the mean, median and mode
- Drafting bar graphs, histograms and frequency distributions

3 Determining the nature of a distribution

- Skew
- Box plots
- Frequency distributions

4 Measures of variability

Calculate:

- Range, interquartile range
- Variance
- Standard deviation

5 Descriptive statistics

- z-scores/ standardisation
- Correlation coefficient: Pearson product moment correlation coefficient

6 Inferential statistics

- t-tests: independent samples, repeated measures, one group
- Chi-square
- Limitations on the application
- Choosing the right test for the right data types

7.8 Frequently asked questions

Will I need to remember the formulae?

Probably not but it will depend on your department. Sometimes your knowledge of statistics will be assessed by examination and sometimes by practical exercises. It is common for the examinations to be 'open book', meaning you can bring in material that might be useful such as a set of formulae. You might be given the formula in the examination also. You will need to find all this out well in advance of your examination. Generally, Psychology departments recognise that they are attempting to provide a practical guide to statistics so they don't normally require students to remember formulae. They really want to know whether you know which formula to use and that you can use it.

Will I be allowed a calculator?

Probably but not one that is programmable. You should make sure of this well before the examination.

How come I've learnt introductory statistics in a social science and I still don't know what they mean when they talk about a margin of error in a political poll?

You do, it's called the confidence interval in Psychology and in statistics. A margin of error indicates the percentage variation (say ± 3%) from the scores you get from a sample given that all the people in the population were to complete the survey.

What's the difference between N and n when talking about samples?

Sometimes you will get a formula that has n or $n - 1$. The upper case N refers to the number of samplings that are drawn from the population. It is just how many pieces of data you have. The difference between the upper case N and the lower case n is that the former refers to the number of your entire sample, and the latter to some set of the whole. For example, if you collect the IQ scores from your class, you might have $N = 334$ (the total number of people in your class). If you then take the average score for the males only, and there are 162 males, then the number in the subsample, or set taken from N, is represented by the lower case n, as $n = 162$.

I've not done any maths except high school. I didn't understand that and I need help with this stuff!

A good statistical technique will be easy to follow, have a clear application, have few limitations and provide readily interpretable results. Most of the statistics you will encounter in your first few years of Psychology will be like this. If you can follow instructions, you will be fine with statistics.

What are inferential statistics?

A t-test is an example of an inferential statistic. This means that you can use the test to infer something from your analysis of the sample or samples. The Pearson product moment correlation coefficient is a descriptive statistic. It describes the relationship between two variables. However, the t-test allows you to go a step further and draw a conclusion about that nature of the relationship between two samples.

Why are there so many different sorts of statistical tests?

Different tests operate on different types of data. There are four major types of variable (nominal, ratio, ordinal and interval) and then two divisions of variables, the dependent and independent variables. Because the independent variable could be any of the four data types, and the dependent variable can be any of the four data types, you end up with at least 16 different types of test. In reality, this gets more complicated because the number of variables can increase to more than just two (one dependent and one independent), nominal variables are treated differently when there are three levels of the variable, and things get very messy once you consider assumptions about the distribution of your data. So, there are many statistical tests that are used for different sorts of data. As you progress through Psychology you will encounter more of them.

Why do we learn all this? Don't people use computers to do it all?

Yes, researchers use a computer to do it all, and yes, you would be mad not to use one. Still, without a conceptual understanding of the computer's output, it is impossible to really comprehend the nature of the information it computes. The best way to get that conceptual understanding is to understand the steps in the calculation. The best way to understand the steps is to do them for yourself without the aid of a computer.

What is the difference between qualitative and quantitative statistics?

The term qualitative is often used as a panacea for all those not statistically driven but still research oriented. Thus, theoretical or philosophical inquiry is somehow seen as qualitative. There are qualitative methods for dealing with observational studies, discourse analysis and so on, but again, these disguise what is meant by qualitative, at least when dealing with statistics. Statistical methods that are qualitative deal with variables that differ in *quality* not *quantity*. So, for example, voting choice is a variable that can be distinguished by quality: different candidates have different qualities (e.g. policies, charisma, etc.). Thus, the choice of a candidate is a qualitative decision and that's what qualitative statistics will represent. The growth rate of infants, on the other hand, is a variable that differs in quantity: one infant is taller or heavier than the next. Quantitative statistics deal with such things. Note that a qualitative variable can be changed into a quantitative variable by specifying an underlying dimension. For example, with voting preference one could quantify how much different candidates are left, centre or right. Then the variable becomes quantitative, statistically speaking. If one were to divide infant weight into 'light', 'medium' and 'heavy', then the variable weight becomes a qualitative variable.

Do I need to show my working in the examination?

Absolutely! See the explanation above in section 7.7.

7.9 Answers to exercises

Exercise set 7.1

1. $\dfrac{104}{96}$ 2. $\dfrac{21}{32}$ 3. 4   4. 13   5. 5   6. 390 640

Exercise set 7.2

1. $\dfrac{1160}{969} = 1.997$ 2. $\dfrac{373}{195} = 1.91$ 3. 625

4. $\dfrac{184}{25} = 7.36$ 5. 1296   6. 14.8

Exercise set 7.3

1. Mean = 54.9; median = 55.3; mode = 55.4
2. Yes: the mean is less than the median, and the median is less then the mode.
3. Yes (see the explanation and answers)
4. 230.2
5. 80 599.21

Exercise set 7.4

1. Mean = 14.51; median = 14.7; mode = 15.4
2. Negative skew
3. 56
4. 61.8
5. 5745.56

Exercise Set 7.5

1. SS = 8749.75; variance = 583.32; SD = 24.15
2. SS = 2187.44; variance = 145.82; SD = 12.07

The values for the SS, variance and SD are all different once the data is transformed.

Exercise set 7.6

1. Reasoning: $z = 0.9155$
   Writing: $z = 1.488$
   Statistics: $z = 2.766$
2. The statistics score is the best score compared to others because the score is relatively rare as indicated by the highest value of z.
3.

$$z = \frac{130 - 136.125}{24.15} = -0.2536$$

$$z = \frac{65 - 68.0625}{12.07} = -0.2537$$

No. The figures are the same within some rounding error. The z-scores are not affected by first transforming the data to percentages.

Exercise set 7.7

1. IV: The type of environment, bright or dim. DV: The measure of weight.
2. IV: The three candidates. DV: The frequency of response for each candidate.
3. IV: Age. DV: Reaction time
4. IV: School status: preschool or school. DV: Rank of preference.
5. IV: Imprisoned or not. DV: Frequency of depression.
6. IV: Order of the item in the list. DV: Frequency of correct recall.

Exercise set 7.8

1. IV: The type of environment, bright or dim. (nominal)
   DV: The measure of weight. (ratio)
   Extension: t-test
2. IV: The three candidates. (nominal)
   DV: The frequency of response for each candidate. (nominal)
3. IV: Age. (ratio or interval)
   DV: Reaction time (ratio)
   Extension: Correlation: Pearson's product moment correlation coefficient.
4. IV: School status: preschool or school. (nominal)
   DV: Rank of preference. (ordinal or interval)
5. IV: Imprisoned or not. (nominal)
   DV: Frequency of depression. (nominal)
6. IV: Order of the item in the list. (ordinal)
   DV: Frequency of correct recall. (nominal)

Exercise set 7.9

	Sensation seeking	Popularity	z_X	z_Y	$z_X z_Y$
1	10	78	0.2716	1.0017	0.2721
2	8	68	−0.2716	0.3339	−0.0907
3	5	42	−1.0864	−1.4024	1.5236
4	7	53	−0.5432	−0.6678	0.3628
5	8	75	−0.2716	0.8014	−0.2177
6	7	68	−0.5432	0.3339	−0.1814
7	12	57	0.8148	−0.4007	−0.3265
8	15	48	1.6296	−1.0017	−1.6325
9	4	52	−1.3580	−0.7346	0.9976
10	14	89	1.3580	1.7363	2.3580
Total	90	630			3.0654
Mean	9	63			
SD	3.681787	14.97405			

$$r_{X,Y} = \frac{3.0654}{9} = 0.3406$$

The sample of 10 students demonstrates a weak positive correlation between sensation seeking and popularity.

Exercise set 7.10

1. Independent samples t-test.
2. Independent samples t-test.
3. Dependent samples t-test.
4. Independent samples t-test: there is no necessary connection between the groups of people. If the samples were random, or matched, it is possible to use a dependent sample t-test.
5. Independent samples t-test.

Exercise set 7.11

1.

Infant	Image 1	Image 2	D	D^2
1	30.2	20.5	−9.70	94.09
2	36.5	14.8	−21.70	470.89
3	40.2	16.5	−23.70	561.69
4	15.8	17.8	2.00	4.00
5	19.5	19.4	−0.10	0.01
6	18.4	25.3	6.90	47.61
7	25.6	20.5	−5.10	26.01
8	18.9	12.2	−6.70	44.89
Mean	25.64	18.38	−7.26	
SD	9.13	4.01		
Total			−58.10	1249.19
Step				
1	−58.10			
2	−7.26			
3	1249.19			
4	421.95			
5	14.77			
6	3.84			
7	−1.89			
8	There was no significant difference in the time infants scanned image 1 ($\bar{X} = 25.64$, $SD = 9.13$) compared with the time the same infants scanned image 2 ($\bar{X} = 18.38$, $SD = 4.01$), $t(7) = 1.89$, $p > 0.05$.			

2. Application 2.7 of Bond and McConkey (2000, p. P1.53) outlines the 10 steps you need to take. The table below may help you with your working.

	Group 1 (X)	Group 2 (Y)	$(X - \bar{X})$	$(X - \bar{X})^2$	$(Y - \bar{Y})$	$(Y - \bar{Y})^2$
1	56	25	2.8	7.84	−5.5	30.25
2	58	26	4.8	23.04	−4.5	20.25
3	54	24	0.8	0.64	−6.5	42.25
4	53	31	−0.2	0.04	0.5	0.25
5	57	34	3.8	14.44	3.5	12.25
6	51	26	−2.2	4.84	−4.5	20.25
7	56	29	2.8	7.84	−1.5	2.25
8	54	34	0.8	0.64	3.5	12.25
9	45	32	−8.2	67.24	1.5	2.25
10	48	44	−5.2	27.04	13.5	182.25
Mean	53.2	30.5				
SS				153.6		324.5
SD	4.131182	6.004627845				

Step

Step	
1	22.7
2	$SS_X = 153.6$ $SS_Y = 324.5$
3	478.1
4	18
5	26.56
6	0.2
7	5.312
8	2.3048
9	9.849
10	Rats in group 2 scored significantly lower times ($\bar{X} = 53.2$, $SD = 4.13$) running the maze than rats in group 1 ($\bar{X} = 30.5$, $SD = 6.0$), $t(18) = 9.85$, $p < 0.01$).

3.

Student	First year	Second year	D	D²
1	1.5	0.5	−1.00	1.00
2	6	0.6	−5.40	29.16
3	5	0.8	−4.20	17.64
4	4	0.9	−3.10	9.61
5	2.3	3	0.70	0.49
6	2.5	2	−0.50	0.25
7	2.9	1.2	−1.70	2.89
8	5	4	−1.00	1.00
Mean	3.65	1.63	−2.03	
SD	1.59	1.27		
Total			−16.20	62.04
Step				
1	−16.20			
2	−2.03			
3	62.04			
4	32.81			
5	0.52			
6	0.72			
7	−2.80			
8	Second year students spend significantly less time at matriculation ($\bar{X} = 1.63$, $SD = 1.27$) compared to in their first year ($\bar{X} = 3.65$, $SD = 1.59$), $t(7) = 2.80$, $p < 0.05$.			

CHAPTER 8
EXAMINATIONS

OVERVIEW

8.1 Four generalisations about Psychology examinations
8.2 Studying for examinations
8.3 Sitting examinations
8.4 Advice about examination anxiety
8.5 Frequently asked questions

Examinations need not be stressful events. If you are prepared for the examination, you should be able to approach the examination with confidence. Preparation is the key. However, the shortcuts you can take should be taken. It would be good to read the whole of Bond and McConkey (2000) three times, taking notes twice along the way (this is called overlearning and it does work). However, you probably need to focus your effort and condense the material, so that the vast amount of information it contains can be retained in some manner.

■

> We are what we repeatedly do. Excellence then is not an act but a habit.
>
> *Aristotle*

This should not be the night before the examination. You want to get a good grade in that 3-hour examination, which could contain questions on anything in Bond and McConkey (2000), material learnt in laboratories and tutorials, and all your lecture notes—including those you cannot find, lent to someone or forgot to take. Below are four generalisations that should help. Following each claim are some steps you might adopt if you think these statements may be truthful or at least instructive.

8.1 Four generalisations about Psychology examinations

Generalisation 1

Introductory Psychology examinations usually contain the following:

- multiple-choice questions
- short answer questions
- essays.

Step 1 Find out what the structure of the examination will look like

- Get a copy of last year's examination paper and look at its structure.
- Examine the types of questions asked.
- Ask your tutor or a lecturer for this years' examination structure.
- Often you will find copies of the examinations online. The first place to look is your university library's website. They will probably have them available in hardcopy otherwise.

■

Failures are divided into two classes—those who thought and never did, and those who did and never thought.

John Charles Salak

Generalisation 2

Lecturers write examinations.

- You will be lectured by several lecturers in your Introductory Psychology course.
- No single lecturer will mark the entire set of examinations from an Introductory Psychology course.
- Psychology lecturers find it hard to keep coming up with novel questions to ask in the end of year Introductory Psychology course.
- Lecturers ask questions in their area of speciality.

Step 2 Educated prediction

- If you know you have a choice of four out of six essays and you have had six lecturers, you can be reasonably sure each lecturer is asking one question (they will probably mark each one too).
- Find out what was asked last year and the year before and the year before. Your library will hold these past examination papers—normally they are

conveniently accessible online. Are the questions similar or based on a similar topic? Some of them will be. Often a pattern emerges.

- Lecturers often make it fairly clear what they will ask in the examination in their lectures, the approach they take or the types of things they are enthusiastic about. (You should attend lectures for this reason, if nothing else.) Write down your prediction during the lecture.
- Share this investigative work with your friends. They will come up with predictions too. Sometimes you can arrange for them to write notes and answers for one prediction while you do so for another. You are not generally in competition with these people and such an approach can be beneficial if you are sitting a lot of examinations at the end of the semester or year. At least discuss with your friends what you think might be asked. It's a useful process because it will help you consider the lecture material and focus your revision.

Generalisation 3

Short answer questions often derive from lecture material.

Step 3 Examine your notes

Examine your lecture notes and handouts for short answer type questions that could be asked. Often tables and figures are used as a summary of something that will turn out to be a short answer question. Essay questions generally derive from a series of lectures, not individual lectures.

Generalisation 4

Multiple-choice questions tend to be derived from the text.

Step 4 Know your text

You must know the content of your text. The Web page has more than 500 multiple-choice questions that you can use to self-test as you progress through your text. It's unlikely that the same questions will appear in your examination since your lecturers will know that you have access to this multiple-choice database. Still, such questions will prepare you for that engagement. Another way is to practice the previous year's multiple-choice questions. Often multiple-choice questions are derived from combinations of previous years' examinations, so if you have studied those examinations well, you will know you have the right answer when they reappear. Be careful, though, as lecturers sometimes rearrange the items so that the correct answer B, for example, last year becomes an A this year. The idea is to know the form of the questions and find the answers that you don't know by examining your text.

8.2 Studying for examinations

> Success is going from failure to failure without a loss of enthusiasm. *Winston Churchill*

8.2.1 The prime rule

Re-runs of 'sit-coms', talking to your aunt, doing the dishes, cleaning the flat, reading your flatmate's chemistry text and popping out for an emergency fuse wire become the most absorbing activities when you are meant to be studying for examinations. You will be tempted to extend breaks in your revision schedule because revision is not a lot of fun. It is hoped you enjoy learning Psychology, but you probably will not like revision after the first few hours. The only way to avoid the problem is to first recognise it.

8.2.2 Create a revision schedule

Create a revision schedule based on:

1. your understanding of what is going to be covered in the examination.
2. a careful study of old examination papers.
3. an educated prediction of the essay and short answer questions.

Find a quiet place where you feel comfortable to study. If you study in the same place each time, you will trigger off study behaviour. However, if you do other things at this place, such as talk on the telephone, play computer games, daydream and surf the Net, you get a negative effect of those activities on your study behaviour. It is not a bad idea to move you desk around at examination time and take away your computer.

Take regular breaks but set a time limit for them. A good idea is take your breaks in the same place each time. If you make a coffee and sit quietly in a designated place, you will not be exposed to so many distractions.

If you find yourself making excuses to extend your break time, have the discipline to consider all the time you have already invested and how making that last little effort will polish it off nicely.

8.3 Sitting examinations

8.3.1 Answering multiple-choice questions

Multiple-choice questions generally have two answers that are similar, one designed to confuse you and one that's obviously wrong. Some hints follow:

- Try to answer the question before looking at the choices. This way the choice designed to confuse you probably will not have any effect.
- Examiners sometimes take one-third of a mark off for those you get incorrect to adjust for chance guessing—find out whether this is true or not. Answer *all* questions anyway. The one-third mark off adjustment will not adversely affect your score and an educated guess will mean a higher than chance score. Thus, you are likely to do better than chance even if you guess every question.
- Move through the questions quickly and return to those that you couldn't get on the first run.
- Never let the fact that you have answered four A's in a row influence your next answer.
- Practice multiple-choice questions on the Bond and McConkey Web page! www.mcgraw-hill.com.au/mhhe/psychology/bond/ There is no substitute for actual practice before the examination. You will get feedback on the areas where you need to revise.
- Remember the instruction that states something like 'pick the best answer' or 'pick the most accurate answer'.
- Often enough multiple-choice questions are poorly constructed and a good student will interpret the question and answers with frustration and confusion whereas a less inclined student will simply pick the 'correct answer' and move on. Do not write out an explanation for your confusion or difficulty. Make a note on the examination questions sheet for later, pick the one the less inclined student would pick and move on. After the examination, raise your concern with a tutor or lecturer.

Advice on guessing multiple-choice answers

- Determine which of two answers look similar or sound similar or differ only slightly: choose one of these.
- Choose the longest answer. (The theory is that the precise answer, the best answer, needs a sentence with more words.)
- Don't ever answer all one letter in the hope you will get at least 25% correct. Examiners do not normally take the time to consider whether there is an even distribution of A's, B's, C's and D's.
- If all else fails, pick a letter as you would for the lottery numbers.

8.3.2 Short answer questions

Short answer questions are given marks for particular information the examiner wants. Generally, examiners only want what is on their marking schedule. There is no need to introduce your short answer or edge around the answer, you must get straight to the point because that is all the examiner is looking for. You will probably not get any extra marks because you provide additional information that is related to the question, even if it is good information.

- Be careful with your time on short answer questions—you can ponder too long with these and cut into your time on your essays.
- Check the number of marks allocated. If it is only 1 or 2 marks out of the total 100, you can be certain there is only one or two pieces of information the examiner is looking for. If there is five marks, then provide five points.
- If the question says 'and give an example', make sure you do! Part of the grade is assigned to your example.
- Choose the answer that first comes to you. Sometimes you can confuse yourself by pondering on a question too long and thus develop subtleties that do not really exist.

8.3.3 Writing examination essays

Disregard almost everything written in the Guide for essay writing for Psychology when in the examination. You will not have time to write a wonderful well-thought out or well-structured essay. It's still an essay but it doesn't need to be well written. Your task is to write in short paragraphs as many points relevant and related to the topic you are given. Do not waste time with restating the question. Put in a scene-setting opening line and signpost an argument (not an original one but one that relates to the question). Still define the points and point to debates. List all theoretical perspectives relevant or competing against the essay question.

- Write a quick plan of your essay on a separate page. The 3–5 minutes this takes will serve you well in the middle of the essay if you get distracted within your writing.
- As a rule, do not write in point format. Apportion your time, you should never run out. If you have to write in point form, do so only at the end of an essay.
- Read the question very carefully! When a question says 'and give examples', make sure you do! A lecturer who asks a question with an 'and' in it will have a marking schedule allocating half the marks for the first part before the 'and' with the second half for the part that goes after. It's surprising how often people mess this up and find they are working really hard for a maximum of only half of the potential grade.

8.3.4 Special advice for examination essay writing

- Support your essay with research, cite the study in the text of your answer but don't write a reference list. Use the shorthand of 'Smith found ...' or 'Smith (1978) found ...'. If you learn about classic studies, they will serve well. For example, you could use Schacter and Singer (1962) at every possible occasion. You don't need to cite the date or any of the authors, but if you can it's a nice way to point the examiner to what you mean.

148

- Guess the topic (see step 2 above) and research a few novel up-to-date facts or arguments to support your essay answers, just as you would if you were writing a real essay. However, be brief and always do this as an adjunct to the fundamental information requested in the question.
- Always write a conclusion—even a very short conclusion is better than none at all.
- Regurgitate lectures! If the question asks for information that clearly fits into one or two lectures, then repeat all you know from those lectures. There is nothing wrong or embarrassing about this. You are under maximum pressure to get out information. Examinations do not seek novelty and rarely will a marker accommodate a novel argument in the practice of marking the examination. The examiner simply wants to know whether you know the basic material well. That is what examinations are set up to determine. Put in the novel stuff as an extra, do not sacrifice the fundamental material.
- Underline key terms, studies and names of theorists when you first raise them and also the name of the theory. Examiners like to say they read examinations carefully. They may do so diligently but you make their task really easy if you identify the key points and make them stand out in your handwriting. It's handwriting, especially that produced in examinations, that makes examiners less than attentive to your examination essay, especially when marking late at night.

8.4 Advice about examination anxiety

■

> The optimist thinks this is the best of all possible worlds. The pessimist fears it is true. *Robert Oppenheimer*

One more generalisation can be made about Psychology examinations: you will have plenty of time to do a good job. You still need to apportion your time but you should not need to ever really panic in a Psychology examination. If you feel yourself starting to panic about the examination, then consider putting down you pen and sitting calmly for a few a seconds.

If you are inclined to panic about time, try this. When you are having a conversation with a friend, stop mid-sentence and, to yourself, count slowly to three. Don't count aloud, your friend might think you are really under stress. Just pause for a 3-second break. It will probably seem to you like an eternity passes. Your friends might think so too because we do not normally have such breaks in conversation, especially informal conversations. They may try to continue your sentences for you—try it out and see if they do. Reflect on how long 3 seconds is in the context of a 3-hour examination. Taking time to collect your thoughts in examinations is useful, relaxing and refreshing. Time only seems to fly by, especially when you are in a panic. Taking 10 seconds out every now and then will serve you well.

Other people can put you into a panic. The person who asks for extra paper after 10 minutes probably hasn't filled their examination booklet with anything more than doodles and cartoons. Whatever that person is up to doesn't matter. More importantly, grades are not given for the length of your essays. A concise answer will score just as well as a longer answer and will free you up to consider the extra points that will score better than average grades.

Get to the examination room early and try not to talk to anyone who might put you off. There is a psychology to standing outside examination rooms that is based simply on people convincing themselves that they have studied the right material or some 'special bit' of material that will get them through with an A. People will attempt to tell you the focus of their revision because they are nervous; and by telling you, they are revising it for themselves. Some especially annoying people try to convince themselves that they know more than you do by probing you about what you have studied and pointing out that you have missed something. By doing this, they feel comfortable, and you feel like a nervous wreck before you have even seen the examination questions. Avoid these people! Either talk to no one or talk about things other than the forthcoming examination.

Rehearsal

It's a good idea to imagine the examination room, imagine sitting the examination, and imagine the finish of the examination and handing it in to the examiner. You might even experience some anxiety thinking about the process but your practise will help you deal with it if it arises in the real context of the examination.

Coffee and anxiety

Caffeine can induce anxiety in people and throw them over the edge of anxiety into full-blown panics. Around examination time, caffeine consumption can hit all time heights; it may not hinder some people but other people find caffeine is unhelpful because it creates such panics. The best advice is not to break your routine. If you don't drink a lot of coffee, then don't start doing so 3 hours before your examination. This is especially true for caffeine tablets and so on.

Even a small amount of alcohol will affect your examination performance—it's not a solution to examination anxiety. The same applies to many other drugs.

8.5 Frequently asked questions

Are examination results scaled for a predetermined pass rate?

Maybe, it depends on your university, the actual pass rate and a lot of other reasons. They are probably only scaled to improve pass rates. Sometimes you will find the pass rates for each course published in university literature or student association magazines.

It's not fair that they take one-third of a mark off for wrongly answered multiple-choice. How do they justify this?

The probability of you getting a correct answer in a four-item multiple-choice question (each has a choice of A, B, C or D) is 1 out of 4. Every four questions a random guess will hit on the right answer once. From the examiner's point of view, the minimum grade for the multiple-choice section is 25% if a point is allowed for each one you guess. But when you guess, you get 3 of 4, or 75%, of the guessed items wrong. Examiners taking one-third off the wrong answers simply recognise the ratio of guesses to wrong answers: 25 right divided by 75 wrong is 1/3. For example, by taking one-third of 75%, you get 25% (the number guessed correctly). If you guess 12 of 100 answers, you will get three correct and nine wrong. By taking one-third of nine, or one-third of a mark for each wrong answer, the number you guessed is three: $3 \times 1/3$ or 1/3 of 9 = 3. You don't get fair credit for guessing so they take this off your total.

What about spelling, grammar and all those complicated terms?

No one will care too much if you spell Freud as Frued or the hippocampus as the hyppocampus. However, they may get confused if the latter looks like hyppothalmapus because it's now not clear whether you mean hippocampus or hypothalamus. Examiners do not read examination answers for spelling, grammar and style. They do not correct examination scripts; they simply assign grades based on content.

There's too much to learn! I can't cope! It's all a nightmare!

None of the above is actually a question. A calm frame of mind is best when studying. You will be fine if you are dedicated enough to read your text, attend your lectures, read this Guide, go to all your laboratory classes, take notes and revise your material. This can be guaranteed.

Can I have a recount, reconsideration or aegrotat?

Check with your tutor or read the regulations of your university for dealing with these things. Don't be put off by the hassle if you think your grade has been affected negatively by something other than a fair performance. Examiners do add things up incorrectly, miss pages or answers and so on. They make mistakes.

I only need 10% in the examination to pass the course. How can I fail?

Some places set a minimum final examination grade. If you do not achieve that minimum, you will get an FFE (failed final examination) or some other equally unattractive mark on your record. Do the work and get the A, you deserve it!

CHAPTER 9
EPILOGUE

OVERVIEW

9.1   On becoming a psychologist
9.2   On making the decision to become a psychologist
9.3   A final note

9.1 On becoming a psychologist

When people ask psychologists what they do, there is often an uncomfortable pause as the appropriate response from the many developed over the years is found. By saying 'psychologist', you often induce confusion and sometimes fear. It might be easier if you were a clinical psychologist, but maybe not since what most people think clinical psychologists do rarely reflects the diversity of roles they perform. Some sometimes say lecturer, teacher, researcher or social scientist but rarely, if ever, say 'psychologist'. Some people confuse the role with that of a medical doctor, a clinical psychologist, psychiatrist, counsellor, and even such things as an engineer, teacher, policy analyst, statistician and professor. Most people fail to find a scheme with which to place a 'psychologist'. A conversation can soon be ended by saying 'I'm a psychologist whose interests include the study of irrationality'. There may also be confusion once having completed your degree wondering what it is that you have become and whether or not you are indeed a psychologist. Even in conversations with psychologists, it is often hard to define just what sort of psychologist they may be exactly.

■

To be great is to be misunderstood.   *Ralph Waldo Emerson*

By the time you finish Introductory Psychology you will know that it is many things. If you reflect on those things you thought Psychology was all about, and what you now know, you will start to appreciate the confusion that people hold when they meet psychologists and even students of Psychology. By completing an introductory course you take the first step to becoming a psychologist. Although there are sometimes laws and regulations that define special sorts of psychologists, in practice most people who obtain work using their degree in Psychology can comfortably declare themselves to be a 'psychologist' (but not a registered psychologist!) if they want to, and with the warning that it confuses people.

If you continue with Psychology, you will find the problem of engendering confusion becomes more pronounced. It is almost impossible to be psychologists without engaging with people, to ask them questions, seek their support, study them and find out what makes people 'tick'. To be a psychologist is to adopt many special sorts of roles. Whether acting professionally or personally, you will soon become aware of the need to carefully manage the way you outline what it is that you do. When acting professionally, there will be codes of ethical conduct and these help define the way you should develop those special roles. How you personally manage becoming and being a psychologist is up to you. The only observation is that such a task may be more difficult than in other professions.

9.2 On making the decision to become a psychologist

Your final grade for your introductory course should not be the basis for your decision to continue with Psychology. Ultimately, final grades don't matter too much–like your high school grades they fade into insignificance with time. Scoring a good grade is important but probably not as important as your enthusiasm. There are numerous examples of people in history who scored poorly at university and yet made significant contributions to science. Psychology is a relatively new science and there is plenty of opportunity for people to make significant contributions without revolutionising the discipline. Then again, you might be just the person to do such. There are also numerous roles for people who develop the skills when studying Psychology but do not refine them with postgraduate study. Remember, provided you improve yourself, your understanding and your skills, then you are doing the right sort of thing. If you find an interest in some aspect of Psychology that you wish to pursue, then pursue it.

■

Imagination is more important than knowledge, for knowledge is limited while imagination embraces the entire world.
Albert Einstein

9.3 A final note

The Web page at www.mcgraw-hill.com.au/mhhe/psychology/bond/ has an 'Updates' link. If you have a general query or concern, then send an e-mail and an answer will be provided. Please send on your questions as they will help others and improve this Guide for future generations of students.

■

Nothing is at last sacred but the integrity of your own mind.
Ralph Waldo Emerson

REFERENCES

Alicke, M. D., Klotz, M. L., Breitenbecher, D. L. Yurak, T. J., & Vredenburg, D. S. (1995). Personal contact, individuation and the better-than-average effect. *Journal of Personality and Social Psychology, 68*, 5, 804–25.

Allen, R. E. (Ed). (1990). *The concise Oxford dictionary of current English*. Oxford: Clarendon.

American Psychological Association. (1994). *Publication manual of the American Psychological Association* (4th ed.). Washington, DC: APA.

Babbie, E. (1995). *The practice of social research*. Belmont: Wadsworth.

Backstrom, C., & Hursh-Cesar, G. (1981). *Survey research* (2nd Ed.). New York: Wiley.

Chater, Nick. (1996). Reconciling simplicity and likelihood principles in perceptual organization. *Psychological Review, 103*, 3, 566–81.

De Joy, D. M. (1989). The optimism bias and traffic accident risk perception. Accident *Analysis and Prevention, 21*, 4, 333–40.

Delhomme, P. (1991). Comparing one's driving with others': Assessment of abilities and frequency of offences: Evidence for a superior conformity of self-bias? *Accident Analysis & Prevention, 23*, 6, 493–508.

Electronic reference formats recommended by the American Psychological Association. (1999, November 19). Washington, DC: APA. Retrieved March 19, 2000 from the World Wide Web: http://www.apa.org/journals/webref.html.

Gardner, H. (1983). *Frames of mind: The theory of multiple intelligences*. New York. Basic Books.

Groeger, J. A., & Grande, G. E. (1996). Self-preserving assessments of skill? *British Journal of Psychology, 87*, (1), 61–79.

Harré, R., & Lamb, R. (1983). *The encyclopedic dictionary of psychology*. Cambridge, MA: MIT Press.

Hays, W. L. (1988). *Statistics* (4th ed.). New York: Holt, Rinehart & Winston.

Heaton, J., & Groves, J. (1994). *Wittgenstein for beginners*. London: Icon.

Kahneman, D., & Tversky, A. (1996). On the reality of cognitive illusions. *Psychological Review, 103*, (3), 582–91.

Kunda, Z., & Oleson, K. C. (1997).When exceptions prove the rule: How extremity of deviance determines the impact of deviant examples on stereotypes. *Journal of Personality & Social Psychology, 72* (5), 965–79.

Lazarus, R. S. (1982). Thoughts on the relation between emotion and cognition. *American Psychologist, 37*, 1019–24.

Lazarus, R. S. (1984). On the primacy of cognition. *American Psychologist, 39*, 124–9.

Lazarus, R. S. (1991). *Emotion and adaptation*. New York: Oxford University Press.

Lazarus, R. S. (1993). From psychological stress to the emotions: A history of changing outlooks. *Annual Review of Psychology, 44*, 1–21.

McClelland, J. L., McNaughton, B. L., & O'Reilly, R. C. (1995). Why there are complementary learning systems in the hippocampus and neocortex: Insights from the successes and failures of connectionist models of learning and memory. *Psychological Review, 102*, (3), 419–37.

McCormick, I. A., Walkey, F. H., & Green, D. E. (1986). Comparative perceptions of driver ability: A confirmation and expansion. *Accident Analysis & Prevention, 18*, (3), 205–8.

McKenna, F. P., Stanier, R. A., & Lewis, C. (1991). Factors underlying illusory self-assessment of driving skill in males and females. *Accident Analysis & Prevention, 23*, (1), 45–52.

Ochse, R. (1990). Before the gates of excellence: The determinants of creative genius. Cambridge: Cambridge University Press.

Polk, T. A., & Newell, A. (1995). Deduction as verbal reasoning. *Psychological Review, 102* (3), 533–66.

Popper, K. R. (1972). *The logic of scientific discovery*. London: Hutchinson & Co.

Robinson, R. P. (1970). *Effective study*. New York: Harper & Row.

Schacter, S., & Singer, J. E. (1962). Cognitive, social and physiological determinant of emotional state. *Psychological Review, 69*, 379–99.

Slife, B. D., & Williams, R. N. (1997). Toward a theoretical psychology: Should a subdiscipline be formally recognized? *American Psychologist, 52* (2), 117–29.

Spearman, C. (1927). *The abilities of man*. New York: Macmillan.

Svenson, O., Fischhoff, B., & MacGregor, D. (1985). Perceived driving safety and seatbelt usage. *Accident Analysis & Prevention, 17*, (2), 119–33.

Svenson, O. (1981). Are we all less risky and more skilful than our fellow drivers? *Acta Psychologica, 47*, (2), 143–8.

Thomas, E. L., & Robinson, H. A. (1982). *Improving reading in every class*. Boston: Allyn and Bacon.

Walton, D., & Bathurst, J. (1998). An exploration of the perceptions of the average driver's speed compared to perceived driver safety and driving skill. *Accident Analysis and Prevention, 30*, 821–30.

INDEX

Abbreviations, 70
Abstract, 42, 57, 58, 59, 72
Ad hominem, 39
American spelling, 49
Analogies, 26
APA Manual, 1, 4, 5

Bibliographies, 48
Bond and McConkey
    Web pages, 4, 105, 106, 147
Bond and McConkey
    (2000), 130
Brackets
    Inserting material, 105

Calculation
    see Pearson product moment
        correlation coefficient
Careers
    Academic psychologists, 7, 12
    Becoming a psychologist, 7, 10, 11,
        12, 14, 16, 17, 90, 93, 94, 109
    Clinical psychologist, 10, 11
    Clinical Psychology, 7, 10, 11, 99
    Counselling, 7, 13, 14
    Forensic psychologists, 7, 15
    Myths about Psychology, 10, 12, 13,
        14, 15
    Organisational psychologists, 7, 11,
        12
    Sports Psychology, 7, 14
Checklists
    Essays, 54

Chi-square, 70, 71
Concept definitions, 24
Conclusions, 22, 23, 36, 41, 42, 60, 72
Correlation, 70, 74, 111, 124, 133, 137

Data, 8, 57, 59, 60, 65, 116, 132
Definitions
    Ambiguity of word, 94
    Begging the question, 91
    Difficulty with psychological terms, 98
    In-text referencing, 29, 32
    Lectures, 107
Definitions, 23, 24, 25
Dependent variable, 66, 132
Dictionaries, 45, 106
Discussion, 42, 57, 60, 70, 72
Drafts of an essay, 53

Electronic resources, 44, 103
Emotive language, 38, 90
Encyclopaedias, 44, 45, 50, 106
Equations, 113, 115
Essays
    Conclusions, 36
    Crux of the issue, 28
    Formula, 17, 20
    Introduction, 17, 50, 144, 148
    Opening statements, 35, 58
    Signposting, 21, 23, 25, 26, 58
    Style, 36
    Why we write them, 17
Et al., 48
Evidence

Research, 28, 157
Examinations
    Anxiety, 143, 149
    Short answers, 144, 145, 147

Fallacies
    Ambiguity of structure, 94
    Begging the question, 92
    Equivocation, 93
    Figure of speech, 95
    Ignorance of the nature of refutation,
        89
    Inductive, 92
    Of composition, 94
Fallacies of reasoning
    Straw man, 83
Figures, 65, 66, 77
First person pronouns, 37
Firstly, secondly,..., 49
Formal language, 36
Frequently asked questions, 57, 77

Gender, 63, 65
Getting resources
    Journals, 45, 102
Grammar, 47, 48, 54, 96, 106, 107,
    151
    Getting help, 96
Graphs
    Bar graph, 66, 68, 132
    Legends, 66
    Line graphs, 66, 68, 132

Headings, 40
Hypotheses, 58, 62

Inferential statistics, 132, 133

Latin terms, 38, 39

Mathematics, 112
Median, 117, 132, 136
Metrication, 70
Mode, 111, 116, 117, 132, 136
Multiple-choice questions, 3, 6, 101, 106,
    145, 147, 151
Myths about Psychology, 10, 12, 13, 14,
    15

Note taking, 107

Participants, 42, 59

Pearson product moment correlation
    coefficient, 111, 112, 124, 127,
    133, 134, 137
Personal pronouns, 37
Plagiarism, 39
Publisher's details, 45

Quotations, 32, 54

Racism, 40
Reading and note taking, 100

References
    Finding the information, 45
Referencing, 22, 23, 28, 41, 42, 60, 157
    Bond and McConkey (2000), 47
    Books, 43
    Dictionaries, 44
    Encyclopaedias, 44
    In-text, 28, 29
    Journals, 44, 45, 102
    Listing, 30
    Pointing, 31
    Quotations, 32, 54
    Web page material, 44
    Participants, 42, 59
Report writing
    Abstract, 42, 57, 58, 59, 72
    Discussion, 42, 57, 60, 70, 72
    Formula, 59, 60
    Hypothesis, 57, 59, 62, 63
    Materials, 64
    Results and Data Presentation, 65
    Sample, 57, 59, 60, 63, 72, 132
Researchers titles, 38

Sexism, 40
Short paragraphs, 42
Significance, 132
Signposting, 21, 23, 25, 26, 58
    Example, 26
SQ3R method of comprehension, 100
Standard deviation, 70, 71, 120, 121,
    122, 136, 139, 140, 141
Statistics
    Over reporting, 74
Style of writing, 17, 36
Symbols, 70

Tables and figures, 65, 66, 77
Theory, 79
Titles, 38

t-test, 68, 70, 71, 111, 112, 127, 128, 129, 130, 131, 134, 137, 138
t-tests, 44, 81, 157

Updates to this Guide, 1, 4

Variables, 111, 122, 123

Web page, 145
Writing style, 17, 36

Yearbooks, 52, 106

z-scores, 111, 118, 120, 121, 122, 127, 133